KITCHEN WITCH'S
guide to
Magickal Tools

PATRICIA TELESCO

Foreword by Don Waterhawk

New Page Books
A Division of Career Press
Franklin Lakes, NJ

KITCHEN WITCH'S GUIDE TO MAGICKAL TOOLS
EDITED AND TYPESET BY GINA TALUCCI
Cover design by Cheryl Cohan Finbow
All photos by Don Waterhawk
Printed in the U.S.A. by Book-mart Press

To order this title, please call toll-free 1-800-CAREER-1 (NJ and Canada: 201-848-0310) to order using VISA or MasterCard, or for further information on books from Career Press.

The Career Press, Inc., 3 Tice Road, PO Box 687,
Franklin Lakes, NJ 07417
www.careerpress.com
www.newpagebooks.com

Library of Congress Cataloging-in-Publication Data

Telesco, Patricia, 1960-
    Kitchen witch's guide to magickal tools / by Patricia Telesco.
        p. cm.
    Includes bibliographical references and index.
    ISBN-13: 978-1-56414-843-8
    ISBN-10: 1-56414-843-2 (pbk.)
        1. Witchcraft. I. Title.

BF1566.T335 2006
133.4′ 3--dc22

2006041922

Contents

Foreword

By Don Waterhawk

This book discusses the ins and outs of finding, making, and using magickal tools. At the outset, however, some people may ask the question: Do we really need tools? After all, one of the main goals of modern spiritual practices is to eventually become the magick (or medicine). At that stage of development people really don't *need* tools. Nonetheless, they may *want* them, as may individuals who have not quite yet manifested the goal of living their faith fully.

Why? Well, think of it this way—to get from one side of a river to the other I could swim. That would mean I don't need any tools to achieve the goal (outside my own body). However, I could get to the opposite embankment much faster and easier if I use a boat, as can the person who does not know how to swim (the boat, in this case, is also the safer option!). Magickal tools are like the boat—they give us faster, better, and sometimes safer approaches to achieving a goal.

While some processes should not be rushed, humans value the precious time that they have. We have a limited amount of years on this planet, and tools help us get from point A to point B more effectively and quickly, thereby saving valuable time and energy. They cut out the proverbial middleman, and become a bridging mechanism between the mundane and the spiritual, between temporal and eternal. And we really need that bridge for more than just it's expediency! Typically, humans, no matter how adept, are insecure. Anxiety blocks magick. Tools help remove that obstacle by providing a little more confidence and turning our attention toward what's really important (that is, the goal instead of our uncertainty).

I should mention at this juncture that anything and everything has the potential to become a tool. I learned this wonderful lesson from a man named Turtle. Turtle carved beautiful sacred pipes, and I wanted him to teach me about the pipe in Native Tradition. The first time he invited me to a pipe ritual, Turtle came out with a little bag, building his altar piece by piece diligently from the bag. There was no way he could have gotten that much out of that tiny bag! This little bit of visual "magicine" certainly set a tone for all that was to come.

We did the ceremony from start to finish—it was wonderful, beautiful, and unforgettable. Afterward I didn't see him for a long time, but then something came up and I went to help him on a project. He asked me again about doing the ceremony (of course I was like a kid in a candy shop). This time, however, I noticed he didn't have his pipe or bag. Rather he pulled out a cigarette and lighter—honored the four directions, and passed the cigarette to me. I stared at him and the cigarette, obviously perplexed.

The question on my face must have shown as Turtle asked me what was wrong. I replied by telling him that the last time we did pipe ceremony it was phenomenal with the endless bag, the altar, and the detailed ceremony—and this time he just pulled out a cigarette. What happened? To which he replied, "It doesn't make any difference what tools you have, what matters is what sits in your heart. My heart speaks with Spirit. If I am not connected to Spirit, then maybe I need to return to those tools. But at my age I don't need it as much anymore. It shows me the way, I can get there…and then I walk the rest of the way myself."

So if you think of your tools, be they fancy or simple, like a road map, you'll begin to see that once you've traveled to where the tool takes you a few times, you may not need that map anymore (unless for some reason you forget that lesson—then you'll have to return and work with that tool once more).

Let's put Turtle's lesson into an example. For natives it's not necessary to have an eagle feather, but that tool magnifies the energy the person has naturally (and in this case in a very specific way: by sharing the spirit of the eagle, and amplifying the spirit of the eagle in that person's heart). We learn how to work with Spirit via a material object to help us make that connection. Now as it happens, it's not that easy to get a permit to own an eagle feather, but couldn't the image of an eagle (treated with similar reverence) work just as the cigarette did?

My favorite tool right now is my lawn mower. (No, I'm not joking!) It keeps my human side busy so my spiritual side can travel, see, and do. The human side has five children, namely sight, hearing, touch, smell, and taste. We spend so much time babysitting them that we can't put as much into our spirits. Thus the tool (my lawn mower) babysits our humanness so we can get beyond ourselves and our perceived limitations. The key is faith, your trust in your tool, and the trust in the teacher, including yourself as the teacher.

Besides faith, tenacity and honest intention are wonderful helpmates. I've been making various spiritual tools since 1989, when someone asked me to make them a wand. The next day I quit my job at the sheriff's department and started doing this full time. That wand was my teacher and guide. It opened a new door. Now, I know a lot of people reading this may not feel artistically inclined or may have some reservations about their capacity to actually try making some of these items. I'll let you in on a secret: I had no idea what I was doing, but I do believe that a lot of the success or failure in the creation process came from not trying to control things with my human side.

Yes, most of us want something visually beautiful, but all the beauty in the world will not replace a truly Spirit-lead creation. In fact, the tool made from our humanness usually lacks "zap" or it has energies that you did not intend, and that are not very healthy for your spiritual growth. So when you are looking for magickal tools or trying to make them yourself, put down your ego and listen long and hard for Spirit to answer. Don't give up after a few minutes, days, or even weeks if that's what it takes. You want that vital connection in order to find the tool or teacher you need, not simply the one that you want because it's pretty. Any time you find or make a tool and say to yourself, "Wow this isn't at all what I expected," that is something truly special.

This listening process also means you have to be prepared to invest some time. The ancients didn't push something off because they had a dinner engagement! If the time was right and the muse was with them, they worked toward that goal. When the muse or Spirit doesn't seem to be speaking, that's a much better time to take a break! In the long haul you don't want to astound others with your tools, you want them to be good teachers.

You may find it helpful to create sacred space before you begin. Many people don't have the ability to remain focused because our five senses (the children) are all screaming for attention. Ceremony is one way of calming the kids, as it has things that fill their needs. In addition, creating sacred space is a tool unto itself!

Three other things that will help make your creation efforts more successful are also the primary foundations to any positive spiritual path:

1. Thankfulness: For your materials (respect your medium). If you're using a fallen tree branch, consider planting a seedling, or going to a tree nearby and saying "thank you" for that gift from Nature. When we are no longer grateful for what we have, we will lose it.

2. Honor: Respect the tool from the second you start making it until the end of its natural life. Many of the tools you create can easily outlast, you and the medicine it holds will affect whoever finds and uses it later. So keep that in mind. Most natives have the tool buried or burned with them so Spirit goes with them (also so that people don't use the tool with wrong intentions in mind).

3. Respect: Never lose sight of what you're trying to do. Have a healthy respect for the energies you're creating and the tool's potential. Go in with a positive intention.

Along with these guides, I would add one more thing: never call a tool "mine." In many ancient languages there was no word for *me*, *mine*, or *I*—everything was "ours." We only own things out of insecurity. The only thing you truly own is what is underneath your feet at that moment (when you lift your foot, you relinquish control). Also, because the tool is a bridge to Spirit, and it can be used for more than just self, how can we say "mine"? It connects us to all things. Think, speak, and live globally.

By the way, don't be at all surprised if the tools you create (or those to which you're drawn) change in style from time to time. You're growing and changing. You're also being affected by life's circumstances. I remember after going to Hawaii a lot of my pieces had a flow to them (similar to the look of lava). When I started gardening, many items sprouted leaves! I think that the more each of us connects with Nature, and walks the Wheel of Harmony (which also governs our creativity and imagination), the more your choices mirror that Spirit connection.

Notice here that I've mentioned people finding or buying their tools, not simply making them. The same heart has to go into that process, and a person should not feel badly if they can't make a particular tool. For example, I might have some idea how to build a ship, but quite honestly I'd rather depend on an expert who will keep it afloat than my mediocre information. And I certainly don't try to make my own eyeglasses! Similarly, your spiritual life is very important—if you don't feel competent to make a tool, there is nothing wrong with going to a dependable, recommended, trustworthy craftsperson or merchant for that item. Please don't skimp on the trustworthy part. I've seen people selling "real magick wands" that were mass-produced in Taiwan!

I also issue caution in buying metal items from Pakistan, Afghanistan, Iran, and similar areas. They have no raw materials from which to make, say, a brass incense burner. Usually the metals come from ammunition casings (tools of war). I don't think you really want those energies in your spiritual life. Magickal and spiritual ethics go with you when you're making these kinds of choices.

Beyond those cautions, just stay true to yourself and Spirit. This book is a magickal tool for transformation. Read the book, tell others about it, make tools for yourself, and gift tools to others. By so doing you take part in a spiritual tradition and potentially create a living legacy of magick that will bless many generations.

Introduction

To do good work, one must first have good tools.
—Chinese proverb

What's in the ultimate Kitchen Witch's tool kit? Begin with spiritual vision, add a pinch of humor, a huge portion of common sense, and some old-fashioned elbow grease and you've got a very good beginning. Why? Because the first and the most important tool in your magick is *you*. You are the enabler—the creator of wonders and the co-pilot in your reality with the Divine. Really, and truly, everything else is simply the proverbial icing on the cake of your metaphysical life.

Having said that, however, tools are wonderful things. They're symbols of something deeper. They touch our being, help us get past ourselves, and act as a support system for our magickal activities. So, we find ourselves at stores and festivals seeking out the best tools. Or perhaps we hop online looking for ideas on making that perfect Book of Shadows, or fashioning a divination system. Then again, some of us are reading this book! *Kitchen Witch's Guide to Magickal Tools* covers all the aspects of our love affair with various spiritual implements—from where to shop to how to create some really special tools that become keepsakes and regular partners in your magick.

Step one, of course, is determining if you want to buy or make an item. The answer to that question depends heavily on your talents and time constraints. This book considers both parts of that equation in the more than 30 tools discussed to help get you moving in the right direction. It also considers economy in either effort, so that your tools fit your budget as well as your vision.

It doesn't stop there, however. *Kitchen Witch's Guide to Magickal Tools* shares with you the rich and often diversified history behind many of the items we continue to use today. These pages share superstitions, lore, and some examples of how to go about applying our tools once we've found or made the ones we want.

For those of you who feel craft-impaired, have no fear. I've made every effort to provide the simplest and most successful methods for the handcrafted items. One of a kitchen witch's central mottos is that a thing need not be complex to work perfectly well in magick.

Just because your final tool *seems* straightforward, remember that your heart and mind inspire the energies therein. Trust in that. For those skilled craftpersons out there, you can take these basic ideas and easily elaborate on them for more intricate results.

There's much more that this book shares, but I'd like to pause here and introduce my photographer and helpmate in the foreword to this book, Don Waterhawk. Don has been a tool craftsperson, guide, facilitator, and friend for many years, and one for whom I'm very thankful. His words will be your teachers, and act as a foundation for all to come in the rest of this book.

Chapter 1

Finding and Making Magickal Tools

In a sense, every tool is a machine—the hammer, the ax, and the chisel. And every machine is a tool. The real distinction is between one man using a tool with his hands and producing an object that shows at every stage the direction of his will and the impression of his personality; and a machine which is producing, without the intervention of a particular man, objects of a uniformity and precision that show no individual variation and have no personal charm. The problem is to decide whether the objects of machine production can possess the essential qualities of art.

—Sir Herbert Read

Before exploring specific implements in detail, there are certain generalities that will help make this book more useful to you and save repetition. In particular, I believe that whether you're going out to buy a tool or starting the process of making one yourself, the most important thing to check is your attitude. If you're tired, out of sorts, sick, flustered, or rushed, nothing good will come of your efforts. In fact, it's relatively safe to say you'll just frustrate yourself or find that you're very disappointed with the results.

I know that sounds like commonsense advice, but our lives are hectic and filled with hasty choices. Even the most adept spiritual seeker is often running around with more on his or her proverbial multi-tasking plate than is reasonable. Sadly, that means our esoteric pursuits often get brushed off, rushed, or penciled onto a dance card somewhere between job responsibilities and household chores. However, we know that enlightenment isn't a drive-through proposition. It takes time and effort. Therefore, because tools are important spiritual teachers and helpers, it's really worth waiting until you're in the best possible space physically, mentally, and emotionally before going any further (and that includes reading this book!).

Finding Tools

In the foreword, Don beautifully expressed many reasons why you might wish to go out and buy a tool instead of making one. In my case, it's simply a matter of being artistically, mechanically, and time-challenged. My using complex power tools is an accident waiting to happen, and honestly I have little free time left in my day already. With that in mind, I've given readers ideas on where to find various well-crafted tools throughout this book, especially those merchants with whom I've had positive experiences.

Now, I don't have personal contact with people who make every tool listed in this book. That means you have to become a street-smart (or, more accurately, Circle-smart) consumer. Just as in the real world, price does not always indicate quality or honest intent. That means you need to go shopping with your spiritual instincts firmly in one hand and a little skepticism in the other.

14

In terms of magick, perhaps you want to prepare with a mini-ritual that helps heighten your awareness so you're directed to the right merchant and tools. Alternatively, you can meditate before you go and really get your goals focused and centered in your heart and spirit. Or perhaps you'll want to make a shopping charm that you can keep with you.

One such charm might include a green or yellow stone (representing money), an amethyst (for insight), and a couple of tablespoonfuls of basil (luck). Bundle these together in a drawstring pouch and add an incantation such as:

The tool I seek is the one that I'll find
In this pouch, my magick bind
And when this basil's sprinkled to the winds
The shopping magick so begins!

Take a pinch of the basil out of the pouch and sprinkle it in the four directions after you reach the destination where you plan to shop.

As for mundane considerations, here are some good guidelines:

1. Get recommendations from other practitioners as to reliable places to shop (including online sources).

2. Shop around for good prices and good quality items.

3. Whenever possible, see and handle the tools prior to buying. It's very hard to get a feel for a tool's energies just from a picture. If you cannot do so, make sure the merchant has an exchange or money-back guarantee.

4. Find out if the merchant knows anything about the item's origin and creation process. This information may help you in making a decision,

especially if you're torn between two seemingly equally good items. Don't be afraid to ask as many questions as you feel necessary. A good merchant knows his or her product and provides above-average customer service.

5. Use caution when something seems too inexpensive. There are a lot of stones that can be manufactured to appear as something they're not, such as jet. I've seen people selling polished black plastic pieces claiming that they are jet and, in some cases, you can see mold lines.

6. Use similar caution when something seems too expensive. There may be a good reason for the cost, such as a lot of man hours on something hand fashioned. I would rather spend a little more to support an original artist or a merchant who's honorable than to take my chances with an unknown. Even so, a lot of people jumped on the New Age bandwagon just to make money.

7. Think long term if financially feasible. One really well-made tool will last you a very long time, but it may also cost more. For example, a cloak with French seams and sturdy fabric is going to bear a higher price than one with simple hems and a cheap poly blend. However, the first item is likely to hold up to a lot of festival abuse over a much longer time.

8. If the item is said to have some type of guarantee, make sure you have that in writing. Register items that have a return warrantee card or online sign up and keep your warrantee information safe for the duration of your ownership.

Making Your Own Tools

We already talked about the importance of self-preparation at the outset of this chapter. Nonetheless, this is a good moment to do a quick self-check and make sure your intention and overall attitude are in the best possible space for magick.

Step 1: Preparing the Components

Once the components have been prepared, the next step is to read over the directions for making your chosen tool. If you're making this as a gift for someone else, your mindset will be just a bit different than one made for you personally. Even during the read-over of the instructions, keep that person in the back of your mind. Focus on your intent to simply be the enabler for this tool's creation, and consider leaving the steps of blessing, consecrating, and energizing the tool up to the recipient.

Let's assume for the purpose of this section that you're making a wand for yourself. Read over and ponder each of the ingredients even as you might a delectable recipe. Do they all make sense based on your goal? Do you have all the components you need? If not, now's the time to find suitable substitutes or gather up the items you're lacking. For example, say the wand instructions call for willow (which is very popular because of its flexibility, representing the Witch's ability to bend and change energy). You, however, would like a harder wood to show resolve and determination, such as oak. Then you want to get a piece of oak, and adapt any directions or wording in the creation process so they all fit together to support your tool's intended symbolism and function.

Step 2: Cleansing

Once all your components have been gathered, the next step is cleansing them. This can be accomplished in a variety of ways, depending on what's safe for your base medium:

- ༅ Smudging with a purgative incense such as sage or myrrh
- ༅ Sprinkling with lemon water (or soaking in water)
- ༅ Burying in salt or clean sand
- ༅ Sprinkling with salt water
- ༅ Placing your hands palm down over the item and visualizing a pure white light overflowing it (neatly displacing any residual unwanted vibrations).

Step 3: Sacred Space

While this isn't a necessary step, it is a nice one. Setting up sacred space keeps all the energies with which you're working right where you want them (somewhat in the same manner as a sink plug keeps the water in the bowl). You'll be able to direct the accumulated power directly into the tool more easily. In addition, the sacred space keeps out unwanted influences.

As with other magickal processes, I recommend you create an invocation that reflects your working. Using our wand again to illustrate, you might ask each of the four Elements to saturate the wand with a specific type of energy (such as solid foundations from Earth, awareness from Air, the light of reason from Fire, and true intent from Water). Also this is the ideal time to invite a personal God or Goddess to bless your efforts by way of a prayer.

Step 4: Assembly

Whether or not you choose to create sacred space, your work area should be tidy and well organized. This has magickal and mundane benefits. The order helps ensure you have everything you need so you don't have to wander away and potentially get distracted or interrupted.

If you're borrowing the concept for a tool from a specific cultural or religious tradition, please do so with respect and thoughtfulness. Borrowing is a very old tradition; after all, if the wheel isn't broken, why fix it? However, we do need to adapt highly explicit traditions so that they make sense in our reality. Keep that in mind as you're building the item.

Beyond that consideration, think about putting together your tool in much the same way as you would a mini-ritual in which you want your components, words, actions and intentions to mesh. Each step of the process builds upon the previous one, and each symbolic element adds another dimension of meaningfulness. Try not to rush, make sure to include all the necessary steps such as using the right glue or properly finishing the surface of the wood, and keep your higher senses open to the leadings of Spirit as you go along.

Step 5: Energizing

In my experience, most tools have a limited amount of energy they can absorb (which then gets used each time you apply that tool in your Craft). Crystals seem to have some of the largest "holding" capacities, fresh wood is "medium," and small tokens, such as charms, hold less. That means you need to fill up your tool's proverbial spiritual gas tank and keep it filled. We will talk more about this as we're dealing with specific tools throughout the book but, generally speaking, practitioners use the energy of the Sun and Moon in saturating the tool. Which one, in what combination, and when the energizing takes place depend on the purpose of the tool. Charging an intuitive tool, such as a personal Tarot deck, in moonlight makes sense; however, solar energy may also be added to keep the conscious mind active in readings.

As to how much time to leave a tool, really trust your instincts. Some people choose an auspicious astrological time and a symbolic number of hours or minutes for the process. For me, my best way of knowing if energizing is done is to pick up the tool and hold it for a minute. Usually it's "warm" to my touch and seems to hum. Your senses may speak to you differently, but you will begin to instinctively *know* when your tool is completed.

Step 6: Blessing and Consecration

From a religious perspective, both blessing and consecration bring the Divine into the process of finishing the tool. If you are a nonreligious Witch, you can probably jump to bonding and leave this step out. However, if there are any ancestral spirits or elemental spirits you'd like to call upon in lieu of a Deity, then you can still move through this step with confidence.

I usually enact blessing and consecration together. The blessing brings in and mingles all the best energies (even those I may have overlooked) and the consecration "sets apart" the tool for its function. You can weave all of this into a prayer or meditation with chanting that supports that function.

I hesitate to give examples here, as your relationship with both Deity and your implements is very, very personal, and the way this step takes place should be just as personal. However, if you're looking for historical context, many ministers have used the laying on of hands and anointing for this purpose. Raise one hand upward to gather energy, and put your other hand on your tool, while speaking the words on your heart.

Step 7: Bonding

If all of this hasn't already created a connection between you and your tool, then there are several ways to build a new relationship. Examples include:

ↄ sleeping with it under your pillow or nearby

ↄ carrying it with you at all times

ↄ keeping it on your altar

ↄ meditating with it

ↄ dabbing some of the oil from your skin on it

ↄ adhering a piece of your hair or fabric from an item of clothing to it

By far, the most important aid to the relationship-building process is using your tool in as many suitable mystical processes as possible. Take note of what works, what doesn't, and what unique insights you gain throughout.

Care and Keeping of Your Tools

After taking the time and effort to make or find something truly functional, meaningful, and special, it only makes sense that you want to take care of it properly. Every tool has unique needs. Amulets and charms need to be reenergized from time to time. Tarot cards benefit from a waterproof container to house them between uses. Untreated wooden wands should be oiled to keep from cracking.

If there are special needs for the tools listed in this book, they will be in the chapter with that tool. Beyond those basics I do recommend finding safe and sound storage for your implements that are conducive to your lifestyle, such as keeping an athame safely tucked away from pets and children. It is likely that you'll feel more protective of some items, and be perfectly comfortable with sharing others. The housing for your tools should make sense based on that feeling. Thankfully, there are plenty of boxes, drawers, pouches, etc. that can be found in most homes or inexpensively at the store. Yes, you could also make a special housing for your tools, but that's not always feasible. Do, however, think about durability and functionality. I use a nice jewelry bag for my divinatory crystal set, for example. It has zippered spaces for my reading notes, casting cloth, and the stones—ideal!

Forever Is a Long Time

Change is one of those things on which we can depend, and that includes our spiritual tools. You may eventually grow out of a particular tool, or seem to lose your relationship with it. You may also pass over and leave a plethora of tools behind (leaving relatives scratching their head trying to figure out what to do with them). I mention these two possibilities as food for thought. What will you do with your tools when you no longer find them useful teachers and helpmates? Options that others have utilized include:

- burning them (or otherwise destroying them)
- burying them with the owner
- cleansing them and then passing them along to another practitioner with a need for them, and appreciation of the time
- putting them into a historical collection
- donating them to charity

How you handle this is up to you, but I would be remiss to write a book on magickal tools without sharing this last thought before launching into individual pieces. These things are truly what you make them—they're powerful implements, and, if made correctly, they'll probably last for a very long time. Make sure those energies make their way into the right and best places.

Chapter 2

Altars

Wherever an altar is found, there civilization exists.
—Joseph De Maistre

While one might not always think of an altar as a "tool," per se, such structures have certainly played an integral role in religions as diversified as Christianity and Buddhism. In part, this was most likely pragmatic—people needed a central place to gather and a surface on which to place the implements of their worship. In earlier times this location was often a tribal fire and a handy rock, but as civilization progressed, the tools of worship likewise progressed to suit that community, culture, and the faith being practiced.

An altar is an elevated or high place on which (or in front of which) religious rituals are enacted and offerings given. Typically, altars were a table of some sort so that they could easily hold the tools required by the priest, priestess, or faithful.

Form and Function

Different altars had forms suited to their intended religious function. For example, libation altars often included a way to drain whatever liquid was used in the offering. Fire altars (where items were burned in sacrifice), including the incense altars of the ancient Israelites, had a depression for safely maintaining and tending the fire. Funerary altars were

often built over a cairn where relics or ashes could be stored.

The symbolic elements of altars varied from culture to culture. In Hinduism the altar of fire represented the center of all things, creation, and destruction. It was normally created out of clay (symbolizing the Earth), and included three circular blocks that signify Agni's fire, the intermediate world, and the heavens. In Hindu mythology, Agni's role was very important. As the God of Fire, he participated in all rituals and offerings during which he consumed the gifts presented to the gods. As such, he became a mediator and facilitator between the worlds.

It's worth noting that there are more than 200 hymns in the Rig Veda dedicated to Agni, and that there are special fire-priests entrusted with the duty of watching over his worshippers. In setting up sacred spaces to honor Agni, the priests make sure the Fire altar faces the right direction. If it faces East, it's an offering altar for the gods. If it faces South, it's used for offerings to the Ancestors, and if it faces West, it's a cooking fire. There is no note about Northern-facing fires; however, to this day the Agni altar is used in Hindu wedding rituals.

In Egypt, Mesopotamia, Greece, and Rome we find highly decorated altars, more than likely in the belief that the Divine deserved nothing but the best artists. Bronze and gold work wasn't uncommon, perhaps alluding to the solar nature of the Divine (many ancient cultures considered the Sun masculine). Besides this, altars often had inscriptions. In Acts 17:23 we read that Paul found Athenian authors bearing the inscription, "to the unknown God." This likely ties into the Roman custom of praying or thanking any unknown God or Goddess who may have been forgotten in invocations.

Conversely, natural altars were more the rule of thumb in tribal settings such as Central America, at least in part to illustrate the belief that the Deity was not only the Creator, but also reflected in nature. I believe the Druids brought the use of nature as an altar to a pinnacle with the standing stone circles and other similar structures.

Some religious traditions took to putting the bones of martyrs into the altar, believing it would give that space special sacredness. Other traditions created special shrines at home or along the roadway for spirits of both divine and human origins. For example, in Santeria an altar to Legba is placed near the entryway of the home because he opens the way to the other Orishas (manifestations of God) and Loas (lesser helpful spirits). Another example occurs in China where people treat their ancestors with great honor, keeping an ancestral altar within the home. We'll talk about assembling this type of altar later in the chapter.

Tools of the Altar

While we'll be discussing magickally specific altar implements periodically throughout this book, it's nice to look at various religion-specific tools from which we might gather new ideas, or minimally improved understanding of the global importance of this sacred space. As one might expect, the tools of the altar reflected its function as did the construction. An altar for offerings, for example, might have basins to neatly hold those items being given to the gods. The Fire altar would include censers for incense and shovels with which to tend the ashes.

In Buddhism we find various altar implements, including a bell, statuary, incense burners, prayer wheel, and flower arrangements. Very often these are handmade items created with as much detail as possible, commonly with gold leaf adornment. The idea here is to represent the beauty of Amita and the Pure Land on Earth, and provide a suitable place for the family or community to pray.

Hindu altars have similar effects. They typically include an image of a Deity or Deities, oil lamps (representing the light of the soul), worship plates (for offerings), flowers (each blossom attributes the good within each person), and water (libation and cleansing), just to name a few items. The exact placement of these items changes sometimes with the Deity represented, or the ritual being enacted.

Moving from East to West, we can look to the Hopi for other altar examples. Most Hopi homes have a room or special space for the altar. Included in this space one might find a sacred meal and water for sprinkling, prayer sticks, corn, honey, shells, and other natural items. Typically, a medicine bowl is also front and center, surrounded by colored ears of corn representing the directions.

Magick

Generically speaking, the altar in magick represents the center point of the mandala—that which is the Circle of the Universe, our communities, our sacred selves, the Wheel of Time, and cycles. As it is typically a four-sided surface, it also represents the four corners of Creation and the foundation or cornerstone on which we build our magick. Consequently, this region often becomes a working surface for ritual and a focal point for raising and directing power.

There are some disagreements in Neo-Pagan traditions as to the proper placement and exact tools of the altar. Even as we've seen in the global community, where the altar stands, how it's made, and what tools lie thereon depend greatly on purpose and the specific faith represented. Nonetheless, there is a tendency to put the altar in the East—the point of hope and new beginnings. In effect, this placement honors the altar as a tool of facilitation.

Creating a Basic Altar

The images in this chapter show several types of home-made altars. As you can see, some are elaborate, filled bountifully with beautiful objects, and others are very simple, bearing only items from nature's storehouse. This makes giving you a "tried and true" altar design difficult, if not impossible. What I can do, however, is provide some guidelines that may help you in choosing your altar's placement, structure, and associated tools.

Step one is very pragmatic. Look at the space where you normally work magick. How much room do you have? That's going to determine how large your altar can be, and in fact you may be able to use an existing flat surface as a starting point. I have an altar on top of a lawyer's bookcase and on top of my computer desk. These locations have several advantages: they are not easily accessible to pets and children, and they didn't require getting an additional piece of furniture (for which there was no space).

Next ask yourself if you can comfortably leave out your magickal implements in between uses. If you live with other people who don't share your religious persuasion, or have regular guests who are squiggly about the "M word," leaving your altar implements in plain sight may not be wise. For one thing, people love to pick up and examine knick-knacks (and that, in turn, leaves an energy imprint). For another, the items could lead to difficult discussions. While I'm all for edu-cation, there are some people who will never feel differently about magick no matter what you say or do. Use your best judgment.

The same advice holds true with younger children and playful animals, especially if you use an athame and herbs in your practices. Some items just aren't safe to leave around unattended. I realized this when I found one of my cats fascinated by a lit candle. He nearly burned his whiskers off! A friend of mine discovered an ingenious solution to such problems in her small apartment. She uses a combination wooden chest/ coffee table for her altar. After she's done with her magick, she puts everything neatly away inside until they're needed again.

The next question ties into the first—where do you want to put the altar? Your space may determine this automatically for you, or your personal feelings on symbolic placement may help you make a decision. For example, if I'm doing magick for loving energies I might want to set up the altar in the South of my sacred space (because that's the direction we associate with "fires" of passion and warm feelings). If my everyday altar can't be moved (I'm not rearranging the living room for one spell), then I might use a TV tray as a temporary altar. Remember what Don said—it's not the item; it's what sits in your heart and your attitude toward that item. If you treat the TV tray as sacred, it is sacred!

Last but not least, what items do you want to place on the altar's surface? Now, most practitioners have special items that go on the altar regularly—such as an image of a personal Deity, a wand, or a ritual cup. This is a perfect place for these items even if you're not using them in the ritual because they provide symbolic value and will also be energized by your working. Other people like to have elemental items placed on the surface in the Four Directions to honor the Guardians and Watchtowers, and then a candle or statue to represent Spirit in the center. Other people still might just roll up a few

tools in cloth and take them out to the woods, sit on the ground, and have at it! All of these examples are perfectly accept-able so long as the result is meaningful to the practitioner.

If space on your altar is lim-ited, you'll want to lay out only those items that you *need* for this particular working and forgo heavier formality. Also, if you feel a ritual or spell isn't suited to a particular tool's energy, that's another important consideration. For example, I don't use lit candles on an altar where I'm planning to commune with Water spirits. As with any type of magickal process, what you use in any given situation needs to make contextual sense.

Creating an Ancestral Altar

The purpose for creating an ancestral altar depends on how you see these people's spirits and whether you consider them interactive. I do believe spirits can speak and guide, if they so choose. But if you don't feel that way, an ancestral altar is a way to honor your family line and have a special place to celebrate special memories.

In either case, a typical ancestral altar has several components.

- Foods and beverages. These include food and beverages that the deceased enjoyed. Some people leave these as gifts for the spirits, or consume them as a way of reconnecting with specific moments and memories.

- Pictures of the people for whom this space was created (a scrapbook is one example). Having visual input also helps us connect with that person's energies and lessons more intimately. For those planning to call on a specific spirit for aid, images are doubly helpful, as are personal items.

- Names. I've seen this done as a family tree, as plaques under each picture, or on paper scrolls. Names have power and meaning. To speak a name invokes very specific energies, which is why they're a common element to the ancestral altar.

- Tokens. Grandmother's favorite pin, dad's tie tack, greeting cards, saved flower petals from a gifted bouquet, a cat's favorite toy—all these things and many others bear the imprint of those we've loved and carry recollections for us to treasure. I mentioned the cat toy because many people do include pets as part of the family altar.

Portable Altars

The last type of altar I'd like to share with you is one that you can buy or make quite easily. There are several places that offer portable altar kits so you can literally take the magick on the road, including:

- *www.ritualmagick.net/altartables.html*
- *www.dragonoak.com/altars/wiccadrawer.html*
- *www.mysticconvergence.com*

If you're planning to buy something like this, I recommend using the Froogle search engine and also checking eBay for the best prices.

If you'd like to make a very simple portable altar for your car, however, it's very easy to do. Go to a craft shop and find a plastic ball that opens in the middle into two halves, such as those used on Yule trees. (I've even used a stocking container from the supermarket.)You can put items representing the Four Elements into the sphere, seal it up with glue and ribbon, and use indelible markers to put sigils on the outside if you wish. I use a little ash from a sacred fire, a feather, a seashell, and dried flower petals in mine and hang it off my rearview mirror. When I want to activate the protection, I just tap the sphere and put it in motion!

I should mention at this juncture that ancestral and portable altars aren't necessary components in a seeker's home unless dictated by a specific spiritual tradition. Rather, this is a way to show our thankfulness for those who have come before us and the gifts they've left behind, or a way to seek and to illustrate our faith wherever we may be. Similarly, an altar itself isn't necessary—the true altar of magick begins in your heart and everyday life. Attitude is everything!

Chapter 3

Amulets, Charms, Talismans, and Fetishes

Courage and perseverance have a magic talisman, before which difficulties and obstacles vanish into air.

—John Adams

The modern Neo-Pagan often uses the terms amulet, charm, fetish, and talisman interchangeably, even though they are vastly different items with traditionally different applications. The original linguistics behind these tokens helps explain why that mix-up occurred. Let's begin with charms.

I believe that charms were the first form of portable magick, being comprised of nothing more than words in poetic form (the word *charm* comes from a Latin term meaning "song"). While sometimes an object was added to this process (like we see with charm bracelets), ultimately, the power of the charm was in the written or spoken word. The key applications for charms included invoking fortune, inspiring love, improving luck, and so forth.

Luck-Invoking Charm

Words and wishes to the winds,
by my will this spell begins
Luck be quick, Fate be kind,
help me in some luck to find.

The History of Charms

People began adding tokens to the charm process as early as 500 B.C.E., specifically in the Assyrian, Babylonian, and Persian cultures. At this point the charms were made of lapis, crystals, and other valued gems often depicting Deities, animals, and people. Each item depicted was meant to portray a certain attribute or power that the wearer wished to encourage in his or her life. This function for jewelry continued for many centuries. It wasn't really until the late 1800s that charms evolved into fashionable items thanks to Queen Victoria wearing a bracelet with tiny lockets attached to it.

It's important to note that charm bracelets are but one form this type of magick took. In Central and South America charms were made in vial form and contained a variety of plant matter or other symbolic items. In effect they resembled African mojo bags more so than what we normally consider charms. Nonetheless, the Peruvian charm flasks were considered very lucky items and were often kept on personal or home altars.

Some charm vials came complete with instructions. For example, a vial belonging to a doctor in Guatemala listed its contents and its purpose. Specifically, it included a brown flower that cured the sick, mild tobacco, and a red bean to protect the bearer from the evil eye. The outside of the vial might also bear the image of a person, such as Maximon (a Mayan underworld deity with attributes similar to St. Peter), San Antonio to help with one's love life, and San Simon to help with financial trouble.

It's interesting to note that I discovered a Victorian version of the charm vial in the United States. This was a small vial typically filled with tiny, multi-colored beans and left by the threshold. The belief was that any wandering malevolent spirit that happened by would get so busy trying to count the beans that either dawn would come and chase them away, or they'd become distracted and forget whatever mischief they planned to make.

A third type of historical charm was one made with cord or paper. This was tied to a person's wrist, ankle, or neck and left there until the cord literally fell off. At this juncture, the magick was released for manifestation. We find examples of this in India, often to protect babies from the evil eye (cords of red, black, and blue); in Israel where a red string is worn by women who visit Sarah's birthplace (when it breaks it releases a blessing), and Brazil where paper bands are placed on the wrist for good fortune after visiting shrines.

Good Luck Bracelet

Braid together three strands of yarn or cord in colors that represent the areas of your life in which you need luck (such as gold for money, white for peace or safety, green for health). As you reach the cross point of each braid add a small charm verse such as "health, wealth, peace—when this breaks the magick's released!" Tie it to yourself and when it breaks, the magick starts to manifest!

I see no reason why the modern practitioner could not utilize any or all of these charm designs in his or her tool kit. The only thing I feel is vital to charm creation is the verbal element. In fact, you really only need words to empower the charm. The other solid components simply add another dimension to the verbal energies.

Charm Divination

A fun use for the tokens that normally go on a charm bracelet is as part of a set that you use for divination. Gather tokens that represent various areas of your life. I suggest a minimum of 13 for diversity. Give each of them a meaning depending on where they land once cast in a four-quartered circle (North, South, East, and West). For example, if the token for love lands in the North, this might imply the need for building firmer foundations in your relationship; South could mean heated passions; West emotionalism; and East the need for communication. Once you have all your tokens gathered, keep them in a pouch and make a casting cloth out of a plain-colored cotton or linen napkin. Draw your quartered circle thereon and use that surface for casting the tokens. Anything that lands outside the circle is not read as part of the effort.

Amulets

Amulets, by comparison to charms, have a much stronger protective focus. The first time we see the word amulet used historically is in Pliny's writings. He uses it to mean "a preservative against poison, Witchcraft and sorcery." The Latin term *amuletum*, however, simply means "a charm." It's no wonder the terms charm and amulet get confused. Unlike the verbal nature of charms, amulets have a physical component (metal, stone, plants) to which the practitioner adds a charm. This was done during auspicious moon signs, hours, and days to improve the overall power and longevity of the item. An amulet's power remains neutral until called into play by circumstances. This gives the amulet greater longevity.

Amulets in History

From what I can tell, amulets were developed on the heels of the charm. The base components to the amulet started as natural items. What people used the token for changed depending on the civilization and era, but the most common ones we find were for health, power, victory, and overall safety.

As humankind developed, amulets began to appear in the shapes of animals, rings, and plaques often bearing symbols and seals that bore magickal power. To a world that was mostly illiterate and very superstitious, writing was, in itself, a great magick, along with mysterious sigils and the names of gods or helpful spirits!

No matter the final images, however, most amulets were worn around the neck or placed in a person's home or tomb. Egyptians, Assyrians, Babylonians, Hebrews, and Arabs alike followed this pattern. The Egyptians in particular had a plethora of amulets including the scarab, which was placed with a person's mummified body to ensure his safe passage to the afterlife.

Akin to the vial charms of other cultures, Babylonians and Syrians used cylinder seals with precious stones as amulets. Meanwhile in Africa, natives simply carried a medicine pouch filled with medicine typically consisting of plant parts. The key here, except when being designed for a building, is that the amulet needed to be readily transportable so the bearer could literally take the magick on the road.

With portability in mind, it's not surprising to discover travel amulets rather popular (in the hopes of getting from point A to point B without issue). A favorite stone for this task was turquoise (used to protect horse riders from injury). Here's an example of an updated travel amulet for you to use in your car.

Travel Amulet

Begin with a small piece of turquoise that's been blessed by a waning moon (so any trouble fades). Charge this with an incantation such as:

As safely in my hands this stone I hold
Keep me safe upon the road
Whether I travel near or far
Spirit protect my little car

Keep the stone in your glove compartment or on your person if you're biking. Note that you can and should change the incantation if you're traveling by air or train (see also the section on portable altars).

The key to the amulet's power seems twofold from this historical review. First, using auspicious timing was nearly universal (with the travel amulet we used the waning moon). Secondly, if the amulet's energies were called into action it needed to be recharged. Sometimes the amulet would actually break from the release of power, and in this case a whole new item had to be fashioned.

Talismans

The word *talisman* means "preservative or protective" (akin to amulets) or a magickal figure (or both). Where the amulet only works when called into action, the talisman's energy is always active, often because of an indwelling spirit called into the item. Traditionally, talismans included specific markings (figures) empowered by an incantation (charm). The most common markings were spirals, stars, mandalas, hexagrams, and other geometrics.

Talismanic History

Traditionally speaking a talisman could only be given its powers by a natural power such as Elementals or the Divine. Thus the task of making them was left to the able hands of alchemists, Shamans, and priests, who designed them ritualistically and then often sold them to the public. Because of the powers involved, it wasn't uncommon for talismans to include precious stones that already held intrinsic power.

In brief review, we find people of Babylon trying to use talismans to altar natural happenings such as the weather. The sorcerers of the Dark Ages inscribed talismanic designs in metal for wearing. More than 1,000 years ago in Tibet, Dzi beads were designed from agate as protective talismans. During the Middle Ages in Europe all manner of talismans were employed in an effort to cure illness (especially at the time of the plague). At the high point of the alchemist's art, the talismans they created as auspicious astrological times were worn prominently by kings and bishops alike! Meanwhile, common folk got their amulets from the local wise person and hung them around the home.

Rabbit's Foot Talisman

It's an interesting aside in talismanic history to see that our modern lucky rabbit's foot may, in fact, have started as a natural talisman in Africa. Here, carrying the rabbit's foot allowed the bearer to run swiftly from danger, which would indeed be fortunate! This tradition was brought to the United States on slave boats.

Modernly we don't see much reference to calling spirits into an item, meaning our talismans more closely resemble amulets than anything else. For our tool kits, the two key parts of talisman creation seem to be the drawing and use of the right base substance for our goal. For example, you could draw a rune of protection in a slice of willow wood for safety in your magick, because willow is one of the woods preferred for a Witch's wand! The wood and the image you're placing thereon maintain continuity with one another, and strengthen the end effect.

Fetishes

Fetishes have some similarity to both charms and amulets. The term seems to have Portuguese roots meaning "to contrive by charm." Sound familiar? As with amulets, these items are made in the image of animals or people (to symbolize Natural or Spiritual forces), during specific astrological phases. For example, Zunis had six guardian animal fetishes for six Directions (North—mountain lion, West—bear, South—badger, Sky— Eagle, Earth—mole, East—wolf). This gives us pause to consider fetishes for our own Elemental markings of the directions in a sacred circle.

The Ancients believed that fetishes had a consciousness, and in turn many of them required offerings, feedings, etc. In return, the fetish promoted the bearer's welfare according to its attributes. Note, however, that this consciousness wasn't quite the same as guardian spirits for a home or tract of land, in that the fetish could be borrowed, loaned, or gifted. Meanwhile, the guardian spirit, called tutelars among the Iroquois, never changed hands.

The overall goal of the fetish is that of evoking a strong emotional or spiritual response in the bearer (typically based on its attributes and what is portrayed). That's why you often hear of animal bones or skins being utilized in a fetish because tribal people had strong connections to the spirits represented by those items. For our purposes, small images of a patron god or goddess might be an excellent adaptation. Here's an example...

40

Bast's Cat Kinship Fetish

This is a wonderful little fetish for those of you with beloved cat familiars. You'll need a small pouch with pieces of dried catnip, either a whisker or tuft of fur from your cat, and a miniature image of the Egyptian cat goddess, Bast. Note that this image can be from a magazine, a drawing, or a small carving. Tie these together in the pouch while saying:

> Bast,
> Cat goddess of joy and revelry
> Hear my words, my earnest plea
> Bless my _____ with good health
> Protect him/her with extra stealth
> And as to my heart I hold this tight
> Keep him/her healthy with all your might.
> So mote it be.

Fill in the blank with your cat's name, and when it says "hold this tight," hold the fetish to your heart. Keep this with you or on your altar as often as possible.

From what I see, the keynote for your fetish creation efforts is the involvement of Natural, Elemental, or Divine spirits as helpmates to the process. A word of warning: do not command such Beings as you might children. Any Shaman will tell you that to do so usually invites all manner of mischief. Rather, work with such powers respectfully.

The Portable Magick Kit

As mentioned at the outset of this chapter, one of the reasons for making charms, amulets, and the like was so people could keep special magickal energies with them no matter where they traveled. Because our society is even more mobile than

41

the Ancients, this is doubly important and useful. So consider assembling a kit that includes several of each type of portable magick.

You might begin with a sectioned box (such as a small jewelry box) into which little pouches or bundles will fit nicely. Make sure you label each item with its function, instruction, and any associated incantation to manifest the energies (as with charm vials). In particular, you'll probably want at least one of the each of these:

- Blessing fetish (focused on your personal God or Goddess)
- Power talisman to support your magick
- Protective travel amulet
- Luck-drawing charm

Beyond those four, think of your daily needs: health, peace, love, joy, and so on. All of these goals can be supported using portable magick. Be proactive spiritually—plan ahead!

Chapter 4

Animal Symbols

Man, of all the animals, is probably the only one to regard himself as a great delicacy.

—Jacques Cousteau

Nearly all of the Neo-Pagans I know have a soft spot for animals: dogs, cats, lizards, birds, fish, ferrets, whatever! This, at least in part, has a connection with our love of Nature and its inhabitants. It also has to do with the long-standing symbolic value of those inhabitants, and their historical use in various spiritual practices. The purpose of this chapter is to take a look at both history (and how it affects our practices) and the way in which animal symbolism can become a functional tool in modern metaphysics.

Animal Analogue

We can go back to our ancestors' caves and find images of animals; in particular those that people hunted. The drawings illustrate the animal as having been captured successfully.

Many modern students of archaeology believe that these illustrations were actually created before the hunt as a kind of sympathetic magick (trusting that doing so would appease the spirits of the hunt). This illustrates the animistic mind with which our early forebears saw the world and everything therein. So it's certainly understandable that we find evidence of enduring animal symbolism tying into magick in every culture and era that follows, and in some instances even a continuity of symbolism in regions far separated from each other.

Let's consider the dove as an example. Greek myth tells us that the bird was sacred to Athena and represented life's renewal.

Biblically, Noah released a dove and it returned to the boat, becoming the symbol of hope and life. In Japan a dove represented a war god, but if one showed up with a sword, it heralded the end of war (and thus an end to death). This type of continuity is something to pay attention to in your own research. As for me, it implies an underlying pattern upon which magick can be built.

The Bestiary

We obviously don't have the space in this book to explore all animal symbolism completely, nor the way in which animals were used in magick. However, one place that we can find a handy collection of animals (both imaginary and real) is in the bestiaries of Europe that began appearing in the 12th century, but often had much earlier sources including the *Physiologus* (Alexandrian book with 49 chapters of theological animal discourse). The writings in these tomes include accompanying symbolic or moral values and some relative humor. One thing seems somewhat universal, however—an animal's characteristics combined with their mythologies to create symbolic values. This value then found its way into many things, from heraldry and literature to all manners of art, including our cunning ways.

Let's look at a few more animals to give us a starting place for magickal illustrations later in this chapter:

- ❦ Boar: Represent courage and strength (especially among the Celts). In Nature, we know these animals are very hearty and difficult to capture or kill, so much is the case that in the language of dreams they often were considered symbolic of the warrior. Meat of the boar was part of the prevalent mythology of the afterlife in Norse and Germanic stories, and in heraldry it symbolized bravery in battle.

- ❦ Fish: These are associated with fertility and knowledge. Taliesin the great bard was found in a fish weir. The goddesses of love, such as Ishtar, were said to feast on fish, and Aphrodite's feast day was Friday, on which fish was eaten in Her honor. In China the word for fish resembles that for abundance, in bestiaries the fish represented compassion and love, and in heraldry it symbolized a generous spirit or spiritual nourishment.

- ❦ Serpents and dragons: These creatures of the land seem to have been an ambivalent archetype. King Arthur was plagued by dreams of both before his troubles began, and of course Satan is depicted as the serpent of Eden in Christian myths. Meanwhile the great mother goddess Ishtar appears with serpents, as does the beloved staff of the great physician Hermes. In heraldry the serpent portrays wisdom (the dragon protection).

ᕥ Bird: These are winged messengers, sometimes of prophecy and sometimes of trouble that's just happened. The Greeks had an entire system of divination based on bird observation. Romans favored eagles (as did heraldry) for their keen eyesight.

It's easy to see where a detailed exploration of animal symbolism is worthy of a book itself, if not several!

These types of symbols leaked into magickal practices in a variety of ways, depending on the culture and era involved. One tribe might eat the heart of a lion to internalize the strength and power of that creature. Another might carry a lion's claw as a talisman for similar purposes. And come modern day, we might meditate on the lion spirit when we seek to know that raw energy on a more intimate level.

Animals in Spells, Rituals, and Meditations

The subject of animal parts brings us naturally into the discussion of spells and rituals (and by extension, meditation). Our modern awareness of reciprocity with Nature and some pragmatic considerations means that today's Pagans and Wiccans have to get a little creative. For example, a South American spell calls for the use of an alligator tooth for luck and protection. Now, no one is going to go wrestle an alligator for a tooth. We could, however, use the image of an alligator from a magazine as the component for a spell that protects good fortune. Another illustration comes to us from Europe where a chameleon's tongue was used for legal success as well as a love charm. Our substitution might be a toy chameleon being used in a charm focused on legal issues in a relationship.

Potential Replacements for Animal Parts and Symbolism

Because we want to honor the Earth's creatures, taking from a living thing doesn't reflect the most positive Pagan ideals. Found parts may be used (if precaution is taken to clean them properly). However, owning certain animal parts is illegal throughout the United States (and some laws vary by state). So, it's prudent to come up with a list of potential substitutions. This is what I thought of:

- small carvings or figurines (these are often found at gift shops in a variety of mediums from glass and porcelain to stone)
- metal charms (such as for bracelets)
- photographs or paintings
- pictures from books or magazines (such as *National Geographic*)
- wood carvings
- product labels, logos, business cards
- beads (bead stores often have a wide variety of animal images)
- buttons and bumper stickers
- toys and games (such as Monopoly figures and plastic barn animals).
- molded candles or soaps
- found animal parts (Caution: these may carry disease! Use proper precautions such as wearing gloves and washing your hands afterward.)

Mind you, of these illustrations for switching from an actual animal part to something more symbolic doesn't do much good if you can't make the mental connection with the symbolism. That meaningfulness is the key to success. Without that connection, you'll be spinning your wheels. While I obviously think it's valuable to learn animal correspondences, that's really only the beginning of our knowledge. To this foundation we should add some serious thought. Meditate on the histo-cultural meanings and ask yourself how those values influence our current perspectives, how they've changed, and how our personal feelings toward that creature should influence its sym-

bolic applications in our spells and rituals. This blend creates a powerful alliance between history and vision that improves the success of your efforts.

Rituals

In a ritual setting, a good time to use animal representations in the sacred space is when you're doing magick for Earth's creatures or when doing special rites for your pets. Alternatively, animal imagery is one way to signify the Four Quarters. In this case, place a representation of an animal suited to the Quarter's Element on a small surface in that region. You can then call upon that animal's energies in protecting and inspiring the ritual work.

There is, however, some caution to be maintained. For one thing, the "as above, so below" axiom implies that a spiritual animal has all the attributes of its Earthbound counterpart—both good and bad (wild animals are called "wild" for a reason). Secondly, think about the combination of animals you're bringing together. Just as some Deities do not play nicely in the sacred space with others, some animals are natural predators for others. So, if you were to put the bear in the North and the fish in the West, you'd best hope your spiritual bear isn't hungry!

Meditation

Meditation is a slightly different equation when utilizing animal imagery. Most often, people meditate on an archetypal animal to internalize certain characteristics of that animal—such as focusing on a lion when you want to become more comfortable with speaking strongly. In addition, a person might meditate on his or her personal totem to develop that relationship more intimately.

Another occasion when you might meditate on an animal spirit is when you feel that a specific creature was somehow speaking to you, and that message or symbolic value wasn't clear. In the following section of animal omens and signs to follow we talk about the odd appearance of animal imagery repeating in your life, and because most of us have little exposure to wild magick in the concrete jungle, it's not unanticipated that you may not fully comprehend the purpose for this visitation. Meditation can help clarify the matter, as may dream journaling.

Animal Omens and Signs

Our ancestors trusted the natural world for many things, including omens and signs that could help make daily life flow more smoothly. The way an animal's fur grew, for example, would indicate what type of winter to expect (such as a cat's fall coat coming in thicker represented a cold winter). The behavior of various birds similarly predicted rain or sun. Insects such as bees were messengers, and other animals such as cats implied good or bad luck (typically based on the color of their fur). The Chinese even went so far as to create an entire Zodiac system comprised of 12 animal houses that cycle around in 12 year periods (akin to western Astrology).

Because many of us live in areas devoid of natural viewing, and even more in apartments where pets are not allowed, we're dealing with a whole new set of circumstances to ponder for animal omen observation and interpretation. It's unlikely, for example, for anyone to run into a moose in an urban environment (unless you happen to live in Alaska!). However, it may not be so unlikely to see images of moose on various items— such as a matchbox cover, a painting, a logo, and so forth. The animal might also appear in your dreams.

Let's say, by way of example, that images of this creature keep appearing everywhere you go. You see one on TV, catch a glimpse of one on a bumper sticker, and see one on a restaurant marquis. That's a pretty good indication that the moose spirit is trying to get your attention. But what, pray tell, is the moose saying?

Well, let's start with basic representative value. Native Americans consider moose as the guardian of the North, the region of wisdom. Moose tries to teach us the balance between gentleness and strength in both word and deed. It also speaks loudly of self-esteem.

So, consider where you saw these images or heard the word moose. If all the incidents were verbal, then consider how others perceive your communications. If you saw the images only when going to work, then maybe the way you're handling your job needs reassessment. See how that works?

If you're looking for good references on animal symbolism after reading this chapter, I'd recommend reading *Animal Spirit* (by myself and Rowan Hall) combined with the book *Symbolic and Mythological Animals* by J.C. Cooper. Cooper's book provides you with a plethora of global interpretations to ponder, while *Animal Spirit* looks at spiritual applications and provides examples from which to work.

Chapter 5

Aspergers

Trickling water, if not stopped, will become a mighty river.
—Confucius

An asperger is a bundle of fresh herbs or a perforated object used for purification purposes to sprinkle water during or preceeding a ritual. Most Catholics will be very familiar with this item (also called aspergillum), as it's used before mass to sprinkle a congregation with water. Similar items have been used in perfume shops and homes to spread lightly scented water (but without religious connotations).

Historical and Cultural Review

The ceremony of sprinkling in a Christian context dates back to about 251 C.E. At this time, a man by the name Novation became Bishop of Rome. His rival Cornelius was furious at the Bishop, because, in his opinion, he had not been properly immersed for baptism. When Novation became ill and close to death, he'd only been sprinkled. Thus, clinical baptism became something of a controversy in the church, yet it was followed by others from that point forward.

However, the custom of sprinkling water either with a branch or another implement certainly was not limited to the church. Here are other examples:

- ♋ Coptic priests used basil branches during marriages and when blessing Egyptian homes.

- ♋ In some Shamanic practices a journey to meet a spirit guide or helper is preceded by the Shaman pouring cold water over himself (or diving into a cold spring).

- ♋ Hindus sprinkle water on their bodies to purify themselves when a bath isn't possible.

- ♋ Thai New Year includes a pouring out of water over the hands of visitors by community elders. The festival typically takes place in April, and the wetter one becomes, the greater the blessings!

- ♋ Ancient Armenians celebrated a feast called Vartavar, which honored Astghik, the goddess of beauty, love, fertility, and water. Sprinkling each other with water was a common part of the festivities; this was one way they showed their gratitude for a plentiful harvest. After the Armenian conversion to Christianity, the sprinkling of water was transferred over to St. Gregory's feast (commemorating the great flood).

- ♋ The Dai of China have a water splashing festival for bathing Buddha (typically held in the sixth month by their calendar—around mid-April). According to lore, a dragon sprinkled fragrant showers on Buddha at his birth, which is what the water splashing celebrates.

- ❧ In the 1300s there was a common Buddhist ceremony called Abhisecana in which a student's initiation is acknowledged by his teacher sprinkling water on his head.
- ❧ Gentile converts to the Jewish nation were acknowledged with a washing ritual.
- ❧ Sprinkling with water was part of priestly ordination in the Old Testament.
- ❧ Boats in Celtic regions were often blessed with a sprinkling of holy water specially consecrated for that purpose.
- ❧ Romanian gypsies pay their respects to the Water Woman (Nivashi) by spilling water on the ground after filling their jugs. One should never offer a drink before observing this rite, or it invokes bad luck.
- ❧ Romanian rain maidens are escorted through villages during droughts. As the maiden is paraded around, everyone pours water on her to invoke the rains.
- ❧ Easter Monday is celebrated in Transylvania by the men sprinkling all the females they meet with water, which in turn causes the flax to grow well. On Tuesday, the girls sprinkle the men. This custom can be seen in parts of Poland and Serbia, too.

As a life-giving liquid, the reverence toward water is easily understood, and sprinkling or pouring out was a perfect way to illustrate that reverence. The asperger, in any form, simply makes that process a little more tidy!

Magickal Methods

Wiccans and Pagans sometimes asperge those gathered in a sacred space for much the same reasons as did our ancestors:

cleansing and purification. We understand that it's easy to pick up a lot of energies throughout a day or week, and not all of those vibrations are conducive to flowing, positive magick. Thus, the priest or priestess dips a feather, a bundle of herbs, or another implement into plain or scented water. If scented, the aromatic typically supports cleansing and/or the focus of the spell or ritual about to be enacted. Rose water in particular seems quite popular.

Making Rose Water

If you'd like to make some fresh rose water for asperging, it's pretty easy to do. Gather some rose petals early in the morning before the sun gets too hot. Simmer these in a non-aluminum pan over a very low heat (it's important that the water does not boil). When the petals turn translucent, squeeze them out into the pan and add fresh petals. Repeat this process until you have the amount of fragrance desired. This keeps fairly well in the refrigerator for a couple of weeks if sealed in a dark jar.

It should be noted that you need not be a priest or priestess to asperge your sacred space. I often make lemon water blend as part of my weekly cleaning routine and flick it around my home (using my fingers), moving counter-clockwise through rooms, when there's been a lot of negativity or sickness. You can also asperge to attract blessings by moving clockwise.

The Asperger Proper

If you want something fancy, you can go to a Catholic store and purchase an asperger. However, I honestly find using a large-petaled flower, a flowering branch (such as heather), a big herb sprig (such as rosemary), feathers, and even a broom all work perfectly well. In fact, Witches sometimes used brooms for asperging to call the rain!

Helpful Hints

- ᔰ Rather than a large broom, use a hand broom for more control.
- ᔰ If using a bundle of fresh herbs, tie the ends together with string in a criss-cross pattern for a quick, effective handle.
- ᔰ Feathers can hold more water than you might expect. Give it a gentle tap or flick before asperging participants or the sacred space.

Whatever you choose, make sure it (a) reflects your goals, and (b) doesn't absorb too much water. Especially in indoor locations, a plethora of water droplets can create a mess on carpeting. Too much water also becomes a safety hazard on linoleum or wooden floors. Mind you, a playful outdoor summer ritual might substitute water balloons for aspergers, but the setting allows for that (so long as the plastic is carefully gathered afterward). I also don't recommend using a bundle of dried herbs for asperging simply because pieces may fly off accidentally when you're shaking it around (fresh herbs are more pliant).

Chapter 6

Athames, Swords, and Knives

My sword I give to him that shall succeed me in my pilgrimage,
and my courage and skill to him that can get it.

—John Bunyan

He who the sword of heaven will bear
Should be as holy as severe;
Pattern in himself to know,
Grace to stand, and virtue go;
More nor less to others paying
Than by self-offenses weighing.
Shame to him whose cruel striking
Kills for faults of his own liking!

—William Shakespeare

In Wicca, a traditional athame is a double-edged blade often bearing a black handle. The two edges represent the way in which our magick can be used for good or ill will (and the sharpness of either choice). However, it should be noted that some Wiccans and Neo-Pagans use single-edged metal blanks, sharpened stones, arrowheads, and even kitchen knives instead.

As one might expect, different people utilize this tool in different ways. Some use it like a wand to scribe the sacred circle. Others use it to cut magickal herbs. Others still place the athame in a chalice as part of a symbolic union between male and female (the Great Rite).

Sacred Blades in Other Cultures

The use of daggers and swords as a ritualistic tool and symbol is not unique to Wicca. As was the case with tools carried as necessities for everyday life, a variety of blades found their way into religious art and customs. For example, Tibetan Buddhism has a ritual dagger called a phurba.

The phurba is made of iron, brass, and/or copper, and it has

three sides. It is used during rituals to symbolize the stability of prayer. It also represents the means to destroy violence, hate, and aggression, and is regarded not in a material sense, but a spiritual one. The handle of the phurba often includes images of a guardian deity looking wrathful, as the blade can be used to kill demons (so they can reincarnate in a better place). If used in an exorcism, both the person from whom the negative energies are drawn and the blade are then purified afterward.

Besides this dagger, Buddhism also uses swords as a symbol of wisdom overcoming ignorance. Ignorance is among those qualities that Buddhists believe create suffering and negativity.

The handles of such swords bears a thunderbolt image combined with other patterns that together represent compassion. Here are some other histo-cultural examples to ponder before making or buying any type of ritual blade:

- Muslim men in Yemen wear ornate daggers often made of silver. The designs on the handle represent that man's status in local society. Anyone found bearing such an item outside of that culture could face serious legal repercussions, even death.

- Japanese warriors carried two swords, a katana (24″ or more), and a wakizashi (12″–24″). These swords

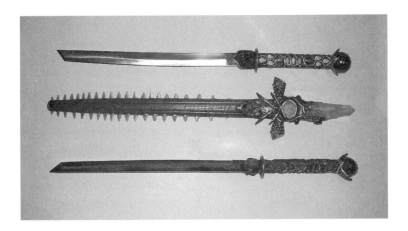

were named for the belief that they literally bore the soul of the warrior. If a warrior felt he might be defeated in dishonor or captured, they would use the wakizashi to commit ritual suicide (seppuk). As an interesting side note, the Samurai followed Bushido, the philosophy of which is freedom from fear. It allowed the Samurai to overcome the fear of death and focus on duty.

❧ In Scotland the sword dance is performed during midwinter. During this, the swords are placed in a cross on the ground (which many believe symbolizes the cardinal points and the Wheel of the Year). The dancer then leaps and dances within the Four Quarters created by the swords. If folk plays are done at the same time, the dancers weave the swords over that character's head, who dies and is magickally reborn, akin to Holly King and Oak King stories.

❧ The knights of Europe were originally meant to represent honor and chivalry, with their sword being a symbol of that duty. There were many ritualistic ceremonies involved in becoming a knight  (or in losing one's stature). The soon-to-be knight, for example, would spend the night before his recognition in prayer, and a priest would bless his sword and armor. To be stripped of arms and your sword broken, however, spoke of criminal misconduct, disgrace, and even treason (the breaking of trust between the knight and his king).

I share this with you because it may well be that you'll end up considering a sword or dagger from a specific culture or era for your personal tool. If so, please keep in mind for what that item was used, why, and when it was used, and if those energies will benefit your magick. If not, you'll want to do some serious purifications before actually utilizing it in your sacred space.

History of the Athame

The athame appears to have been most predominant in Cabbalistic writings and other tomes of High Magick. For example, the 1914 translation of the Key of Solomon (by deLaurence) speaks of a black-handled knife for making the Circle. It goes on to instruct that such a tool must be constructed during the hour of Saturn, on the day of Mercury, tempered three times by fire and dipped in black cat's blood and hemlock juice. No, not appealing to me either! But the idea, apparently, was to make something that spirits would fear, especially baneful ones. This concept seems to be mirrored in a 1500s woodcut that shows a Witch controlling demons with nothing more than a bundle of herbs and a dagger.

However, trying to pin down when athames became common among workers of the Craft, and even where or when the word originates proves difficult. We know that a tome called the *Clavicle of Solomon* from the 1500s speaks of a knife called an arthana. This word may be close enough to garner linguistic connections, but that's a best guess.

Making Your Athame

As you can see from the pictures, an athame can become an item of infinite beauty and complexity. However, any good Kitchen Witch will tell you that even a steak knife can be a sacred tool if used with respect and intent. For those who do not feel you have the ability to make a blade using the instructions in this chapter, this is good news indeed. Realistically, you can even decorate a butter knife and have it work effectively (and for Witches with young children, this is a doubly pragmatic choice for safety reasons—kids just love to grab for knives!). You can also buy wonderfully crafted items such as these from the people at *www.waterhawkcreations.com*, who I

61

personally know and trust for quality handmade, insightful products.

Metal Athame Instructions

Step One: Begin with a piece of steel. A metal blank would be nice, but if need be you can even use an old file. Next, heat the steel until it turns red. You can use a propane flame, or even your gas stove, but be aware that the less powerful the flame the longer it will take to heat the metal (several hours by stove). You'll be letting it cool afterward. This process simply makes the steel a little less hard to shape.

Step Two: Mark the metal, outlining the shape you want for your athame. Remember to leave a handle section (the tang) that's thinner but equal in length to your athame blade (this provides balance and stability).

Using some type of saw fashioned for metal, cut out that image. File the edges so you don't cut yourself. You may want to wear protective eye and hand coverings during this part in case metal goes flying or you get a sharp edge.

Step Three: Using rough files or a grinding wheel, smooth out your edges to the point where you're happy with them. The last bit of smoothing can be done with wet and dry sandpaper in ever-increasingly fine grades.

Step Four: Tempering—heat up the blade again until its red hot (hotter than the first time). At this juncture you'll need to dip the blade into luke-warm water (using pliers to protect your hand). Let this cool and wipe it clean.

Heat it again to the dull red temperature of the first heating, and move it to the water a second time. Clean. Now, on the third heating you're watching for the blade's color to go from pale yellow to a darker yellow (straw). Make sure to heat evenly and keep the point farthest away because it won't take as long for that part to reach the right temperature. When it reaches the second, darker yellow, dip it again in water, and let it cool. The blade is complete except for the handle and any magickal processes you desire.

Step Five: To make the handle, pick out two pieces of wood (symbolic if you wish). Lay the tang of the blade on the wood and outline it. You'll want to carve out a space on each piece of wood so that they'll fit around it snugly and connect. I use a wood awl for this purpose as it's comfortable in my hand and provides great control. Go slowly! You don't want to take out too much or the blade will not be secure in the handle. When the pieces of wood lay together flatly with the tang between them—just open it up, add epoxy to both sides, put the tang

back in its nest, and lay the final piece of wood on top. You'll want to clamp this until dry—the clamp helps the glue spread evenly. Do not touch for three days (if you time this right, it could be the three days of a full moon!).

Final Touches: At this point some people add leather wrappings to the handle, others carve the wood with meaningful symbols, and some just bless and charge the tool.

As with any tool, an athame is an extension of self in the magick Circle. It can help us center, banish, evoke, and command, though for High Magick we don't see a lot of evoking and commanding these days. However, most practitioners feel it's important to develop a relationship with one's athame even to the point where it's considered a breach of magickal etiquette to touch another person's blade without permission. This is a good piece of insight to carry with you, especially at public gatherings where community altars may be set up.

Chapter 7

Bells

The bells discuss the hour's gradations,
Dusty shelves hold prayers and proofs:
Above, Chaldean constellations
Sparkle over crowded roofs.

—Philip Larkin

Bells are hollow vessels (typically of metal) that when hit with an interior or exterior hammer, produce a ringing sound. Note, however, that bells can be made of horn, clay, glass, and even wood, and utilize a clapper or mallet as the sounding device. So, even a drinking glass to which one applies a metal spoon effectively becomes a bell by definition (and is certainly a viable substitute for those practitioners who wish an inexpensive and effective option).

Ringing Out History

Humans have used bell-like items since the dawn of civilization. At this juncture, people pounded on various noise-makers, using them to run off malevolent spirits or announce important festivals. Come the Bronze Age in China, something far more sophisticated developed in metal. It wasn't until the medieval era that we begin to see the development of bells as we now think of them (with the downward hanging mouth and distinctive curves). Hanging the bell in this way allowed it to swing and release a louder, full-bodied sound.

One of the first written records of bells being added to sailing ships was in 1485 on a ship called Grace Dieu. The usefulness of this item for keeping track of time evidenced itself about a decade later when the inventory for regent ships from England typically included two watch bells! The duty of sounding the bells was often that of a boy who watched an hourglass and struck a bell when the sand ran out, then turned the hourglass again.

During the 16th century, bell-ringing was mostly a task left to squires or nobles. In fact, the very first bell-ringer society was founded by Sir William Brereton in 1637. Beyond this, bells became a tool for ringing out warnings to seafaring ships during poor weather. Various captains' logs from the 1600s to the late 1800s speak about ringing bells during fog, and by 1858 the British Navy made this action mandatory as a safety precaution.

While bells made some religious inroads during the Middle Ages in both Christian and Buddhist settings, this implement didn't become strongly associated with the church until the 1800s when they began to be hung in churches to herald services and other religious events regularly. This transition, along with improvements in bell making, allowed (and encouraged) women to begin bell-ringing by around 1900.

Bell Superstitions and Symbolism

Bells are another implement that seem to have accrued a large body of superstition and lore, some of which provide us with ideas on applying this tool in magickal practices. Here are just a few examples:

- The sound of bells drives away demons because they're afraid of the loud noise. This belief was common in many settings, including Europe, China, and the Balkans. Some practitioners use a bell as part of invoking the Quarters, or as an implement to help banish negative energies.

- The Jews, Egyptians, Assyrians, and Copts alike all wore bells as amulets (often engraved with figures of Deities to improve their effectiveness). This gives rise to considering bells as parts of modern amulets, charms, and talismans.

- When a bell rings, a new angel has received his or her wings. For our purpose, this might translate into using bells as part of blessing spells and rituals.

- Ringing church bells during thunderstorms is said to keep the area safe from lightning. This would correspond to using a bell in protective magick, to "sound out" the release of energy, and purpose toward the intended goal.

- Siberian Shamans wore bells while delivering incantations and prophesies, feeling the sound kept away unwanted intrusion from unhelpful spirits. Similarly, among the Ashanti, mothers put iron bells on the ankles of an ailing child to drive away the spirit of sickness (more examples of shielding magick).

- Valuable or useful animals around the world (such as sheep, cows, goats, camels, elephants, donkeys, and horses) often bore bells to guard them from thievery and keep them healthy.
- The Chinese rang bells during droughts to call the rain. This provides some basis for using bells in weather magick.
- European farmers circled their fields while ringing bells to ensure a plentiful harvest. This ties into rites for fertility and abundance, in which bells also played a role in a variety of regions.

In terms of symbolism, Buddhism sees the sound of a bell as representing perfect wisdom. The Tantric subsect of Buddhism considers a bell to represent the feminine principle. In China it's an emblem of respect, faithfulness, and vigilance—so much so that the ringing of a bell at weddings signals the oneness of the bride and groom. In some settings, such as ancient Israel, women wore bells until their wedding day to signify their purity. And among Hindus and the Teutonic peoples bells signaled a person's rank or nobility in life (likely due to the fact that metal bells were costly and rare).

Bells in Religion and Magick

I spoke briefly of the Christian church and bells at the outset of this chapter. But what of other faiths? It seems that a bell was a popular tool in many settings. A beautiful bell from Assyria dated to about 600 B.C.E. bears images of three gods (and may have been used in worship of those Beings). Babylonian people used bells to welcome the seasons as part of their annual rituals. In Confucian temples, bells sound out between readings of hymns, binding the ritual together in literal and symbolic harmony. Other examples of bells in world religion include:

- ❧ Peru: Aborigines greet their Gods with bells.

- ❧ Egypt: Feasts for Osiris began with the sounding of bells.

- ❧ Afro-Asiatic: Bells regularly accompanied Coptic chants.

- ❧ India: Hindu priests use bells in prayers to Shiva.

- ❧ Africa: Priests call upon the Gods with bells and dance.

- ❧ Native American: Bells adorn the costumes for various tribal rituals.

- ❧ Tibet: Buddhist monks use a gong (a flat, disk-shaped bell) as a call to prayer or meditation (and sometimes a tool for centering one's focus).

- ❧ Israel: Bells appear on the hem of the High Priest's temple robes.

- ❧ Bhutan monks and nuns accompany rituals with hand bells, temple bells, and gongs.

- ❧ Medieval Europe: Clerics regularly rang bells at funerals in the hopes of keeping angry spirits from wandering about.

- ❧ China: Buddhists chant in rhythm to the sounding of bells, each stroke ringing out the name of the Buddhas inscribed thereon.

- ❧ Shakers: Bells were a sacred tool that often accompanied chanting (specifically for healing rituals).

- ❧ Rome (post-Constantine): Christian churches hung bells outside and priests tolled at the appointed hours (which also helped local people know the time!).

Spiritually speaking there is no question that the ringing of a bell releases vibrations, and there's no reason that a practitioner cannot use those sounds to indicate or announce intention. Among Wiccans, I've seen bells used to:

- ❧ Welcome the Divine (or invoke Him or Her), often after the lighting of a God or Goddess candle or reciting a prayer or invocation.

- ❧ Signal the release of a Circle after releasing the Quarters.

- ❧ Symbolize the Feminine/Yin (a womb), much as a cup or bowl does.

- ❧ Improve meditative focus or toning/chanting efforts (steadily ringing throughout the activity).

- ❧ protect a space (in this case, the bell isn't always sounded but simply hung nearby. An alternative to a bell is a set of wind chimes empowered to ring out when trouble looms.

- ❧ Denote an important moment in a ritual (such as when the cone of power is being released, or when a couple is declared married).

They are also employed as spell components (often appearing in the incantation, and rung when indicated in the spell's directions). In this case I recommend using a bell according to the symbolic value(s) to which you best relate. If you think of a ringing bell as sounding warnings, for example, then add this tool to protective and proactive spells.

Banging Out a Bell?

The basic tools for making metal bells include sheet metal shears, a hydraulic press, lathe, vertical mill, drill press, hand tools, and an acetylene torch. This puts making a metal bell outside most practitioner's skill sets or budget. There are, however, some alternatives. For example, find several different ceramic or clay cups. Tap on them gently with a piece of wood or metal to determine if you like the way they sound. If you find one that seems particularly pleasing, you can either suspend a clapper on the inside center of the cup with a string using ceramic glue, or small craft bells likewise suspended. You will similarly have to glue a string to the bottom, outside-center of the cup so you can hang it. If you want to use it as a hand bell, try gluing a piece of plastic straw securely there instead, then gather up the two ends in your fingers as a handle.

To be honest, I've found these types of bells less than personally pleasing, but it is a fun craft project for children. A second option is to hollow out a piece of wood. You can do this with wood-working tools, carving implements, and sand paper. The trick here is that different types of woods make different sounds depending on the thickness of the "bowl" you've created. You'll want to test the resonance throughout the carving process so you get a sound you like.

Note that you also will want to put a small hole in the center top of the wooden bell from which to suspend a clapper (wood against wood seems to make a more pleasing sound than metal against wood). However, as before, the type of wood, and the size and shape of the clapper changes the tone. So this type of bell requires patience to complete. The benefit, however, is that the wood can easily be decorated with carvings, burnings, or paintings that designate your magickal purpose.

Now, I'm no wood worker, and certainly not a metalsmith. So, I like using good water glasses and simply tapping them with a piece of silverware. Just by adding various amounts of water to the glass I can adjust the tone. Better still, this tool can then multi-task in the magickal working by being either a libation cup or beverage chalice!

Chapter 8

Books of Shadow and Grimoires

Books are never far from a scholar's hands, just as songs are never far from a singer's lips.

—Chinese proverb

A Book of Shadows (BOS), or Grimoire, is a gathering of magickal spells, incantations, herbals, and symbols with instructions for how to utilize each. If you think of it as a cookbook for magick, with additional ritualized elements, you'll get the idea. The word *Grimoire* comes from the Old French *Gramaire*, meaning occult learning or knowledge. During the 14th to 15th century it also meant grammar (possibly due to the superstitions surrounding the power of written words because so few people were literate).

Bookmark: History

Around 3500 B.C.E., Sumerians began using the Cuneiform alphabet on clay tablets. Come 2500 B.C.E., scrolls were being used (with papyrus following around 2400 B.C.E.). In 196 B.C.E. the Rosetta Stone was cut, followed by the advent of paper in China in 150 C.E. And finally the Gutenberg press came on the scene in 1450, changing the face of writing (and books) forever.

As the ways in which people kept information changed, so did their outlooks about the written word. Books were expensive; people who could write were rare. So it's not surprising to find various mages and sages using books to carefully note their formulas. From complex instruction for invoking demons and banishing curses, Grimoires appeared quite commonly between the 12th and 18th centuries. Now, some modern scholars feel that some of the wording in these books was really a code, in-

tended to fool those who should not be tinkering with such power haphazardly. That doesn't surprise me, especially coming from people who often felt there was a limited amount of magick in the world. What is surprising is the amount of Christian verbiage in these tomes. Reference to prayer, God, Jesus, and angels dotted the texts liberally, perhaps as an attempt to live cooperatively with the predominant religious power.

During this time we find two types of manuals. The first is that of natural magick or head Witchery (what would be considered the magick of common folk documented by historians, physicians, and similar studied observers of human behavior).

These collections typically include a lot of herbal formulas (especially for health, be it human or animal, and fertility, be it personal, animals, or the garden!). Other common instructions were charms to improve wealth, protect, and obtain favors, be they personal or legal.

The second type of book was far more formal and detailed, what we would consider High Magick. Such collections include sigils, invocations, and even the use of "heavenly" or magickal languages. One example of this is the Lemegeton (also known as the Key of Solomon). Legend has it that Solomon himself authored this text, while it only came into public notice in the 12th century. The Lesser Key of Solomon (Ars Goetia) dating from the 16th century includes a list of spirits, their powers, and exactly how to invoke them. Obviously, a very different focus from the hearthside collections.

For those readers who would like to see some of the older Grimoires first hand, there are several online resources (About.com is a good starting place) and at least one CD collection available at *www.lifetechnology.org/grimoires.htm*.

In particular check out the following titles:

- ତ୍ୟ *Natural Magick* by John Babtista Porta
- ତ୍ୟ *Magical Elements* (1655)
- ତ୍ୟ *Key of the Mysteries* by Eliphas Levi
- ତ୍ୟ *Ancient Book of Formulas* by Lewis de Claremont
- ତ୍ୟ *Three Books of Occult Philosophy* by Agrippa
- ତ୍ୟ The *Sefer Yetsirah* (very important in Cabbalism), typically attributed to Rabbi Akiba ben Joseph
- ତ୍ୟ The *Hieroglyphic Monad* by Dr. John Dee

In recent history there has been a rebirth of Grimoires, thanks greatly to the New Age publishing industry and increased continuity in various magickal groups (some of whom now pass along Books of Shadows to their adherents). In addition,

75

many practitioners like to create a personal Book of Shadows that includes their favorite tidbits of metaphysical information.

By the Book

Personal Books of Shadow come in many shapes and forms. Some people use three-ring binders. Others purchase a pre-bound blank book. Others (like me) still use their computer as a virtual Grimoire. In determining what form your Book of Shadows will take in terms of both complexity and medium, I recommend considering the following:

1. Time constraints: Making your own paper and ink, or even going so far as to bind your own book, will take much more time than beginning with a pre-fabricated blank book of some sort

2. Household: Pets and children love to play with beautiful things. If you put many hours of work into a BOS, you won't want it covered in jelly or paw prints. Thus, ask yourself if you either have a safe storage place or, if you hope to make this a centerpiece, if that area will be far away from unwanted paws and hands.

3. Size: Our faith is by nature something that grows and transforms as we have more experience on which to fashion our methods. This means your BOS will grow throughout your lifetime, and may even turn into several Grimoires. Choose your medium so it reflects that potential growth comfortably.

4. Lifestyle: If you travel a lot, you may want one "portable" BOS and another of a more permanent nature that stays safely at home. This is where the virtual laptop Grimoire comes in very handy (you can also process your notes here until you're happy

with them before transferring into the permanent fixture.

5. Inclusive material: Most people have a lot of sections to their Book of Shadows and even sub-sections. These might include, but are not limited to:

    - Gods and Goddesses
    - Tools and Functions
    - Invocations
    - Chants
    - Spells
    - Amulets and Charms
    - Holidays
    - Meditations
    - Quotes and Sayings
    - Personal Journal
    - Herbalism
    - Trees and Flowers
    - Animal Symbolism
    - Kitchen Witchery
    - Signs and Sigils
    - Color Symbolism
    - Divination
    - Number Symbolism
    - Astrology
    - Magickal Gardening

And that's just the tip of the iceberg! When you're assembling a book with sections, you want a medium that will be flexible to such a configuration (this is one reason why three-ring binders have become relatively popular).

So even a simple personal BOS requires some forethought. And don't think for a minute that just because your book is "simple" that it has to lack personal flair. I've seen people personalize their three-ring binder Grimoires by:

- Adding aromatics to various sections (dabbing oil on paper).
- Using unique inks, markers, and crayons or typed fonts.
- Pressing flowers into the pages.
- Adding photographs or other cut and paste illustrations.
- Decoupage on the cover (or other artistic efforts).
- Color coding the paper elementally or thematically.

For those individuals who want something even a little more specialized, I offer these ideas. First, how about making your own paper? For one sheet of finished paper, you'll need a bunch of scrap paper (at least enough to equal two full sheets of your evening newspaper). You will also need a craft blender (one you don't use for food), 2 tablespoons of white glue, 2 1/2 cups of water, old panty hose, a coat hanger, and an iron.

Fill the kitchen sink with 4 inches of water. Bend the coat hanger into the external size and shape that you want your paper to be when its finished. Stretch the panty hose over that frame until taught (but make sure there are no holes). You may wish to make several covered frames so you can make more than one piece of paper at a time (which will mean increasing your recipe accordingly—this is for one sheet of finished paper).

Next, put about one third of the scrap paper into the blender with just a little water. Chop on high. Continue adding paper and water until mixed well and for at least three more minutes afterward, during which time you add the glue. If you wish, now is the time to personalize your paper a little bit by adding glitter, hair, aromatic oils, food coloring, lace, finely ground herbs or flowers, ribbon, or feathers. Note that you may wish to consider the symbolic value of any item you add to your paper in terms of how it will amplify the energies in your Book of Shadows.

Third, put your frames in the bottom of the sink which is already filled with water, then add the paper mixture. Slowly lift each frame through the fiber. You want a nice even covering. Put this aside on several sheets of paper to dry, or hang them off the clothes line in the sun. Once dry, the paper peels off of the frame with ease. Now you can iron it to get a more even writing surface. However, do not use for at least 48 hours after ironing, as the heat helps remove any residual water from the paper.

Take the pulp remnants outside or flush them down the toilet. I use a large ladle or bowl to get this out of the sink. I also rinse the blender outside. This avoids the potential of clogging your pipes.

Think Ink?

If you've made your own paper, what about ink? Native Americans and Europeans used a wide variety of natural items to create ink including decoctions of pokeweed, elderberry, and hollyhock! If you're feeling secretive, write in lemon juice (which dries invisible until you heat it up!). And if you want some scent-ual appeal, add 10 drops of blended essential oils to a pre-purchased bottle of ink so your book becomes an exercise in aromatherapy!

Don't stop there! Add drawings and photographs where they help illustrate your point or goal. If you're an artist, this is doubly meaningful. I do, however, suggest fixing any pencil drawings with a light coating of skim milk.

If you want your BOS to take a walk on the wild side, press components, herbs, or flowers for that part of your tome so that they become a ready ingredient. It's pretty easy to do. I keep an old book around just for this purpose. Pick flowers, leaves, or herbs when dry and clean them of any dirt. Put the chosen plant equally spaced on a paper towel and fold the towel over (envelope style). Put this into the book in the middle, and put another heavy item on top. In about six weeks it will be ready to transport into your Grimoire. Just one word of caution—plants do become crumbly over time, so you may want to consider waxing the item or adding a preservative spray.

Last, but not least, leave room for a little whimsy in your BOS—magick should be fun, and bring a smile to your face. Add a little glitter, bits of sand, greeting cards from Circle-mates, tickets from festivals, and so on. to these pages. This book is very much a spiritual diary that doubles as a reference text. Let it reflect the fullness and richness of your spiritual adventure!

Chapter 9

Bowls, Cups, and Chalices

Eat your meals according to the size of your bowl

—Chinese proverb

There lies intact that chalice of ours,
And its presence adds to the rhyme of love
Persistently sung by the fall above.
No lip has touched it since his and mine
In turns there from sipped lover's wine.

—Thomas Hardy

Magickal practitioners often use a cup, bowl, or chalice on the sacred altar to represent the Feminine Divine (because of the womb shape). These implements often hold libations, offerings, incense, and spell components from a purely practical perspective. However, in looking at numerous histo-cultural settings, we are certainly not alone in using this tool. Let's take a brief look at the history behind the symbolism of bowls and cups. In so doing, bear in mind that it's difficult to separate vessels from the sacred beverages they held and the myths of the gods that speak of wine, beer, milk, and other drinks. I will, however, cover more about beverages in the chapter on potions.

When Is a Bowl Not a Bowl?

The earliest drinking vessels (other than the human hand) included gourds, horns, and shells. Asians and Africans created bowls of wood and metal, and later they joined other cultures who decorated such implements with precious gems. Historians believe that the first actual goblet, however, came out of the Mediterranean region, some even being made in crude glass.

From a philosophic and religious perspective, we begin in Tibet where crystal and brass bowls are not simply decorative—they sing! People believe the music created by the bowls brings positive chi into any environment and clears away negativity. One thing the Tibetan bowl holds in common with Wicca is that it represents the Yin force of the universe. Spaces that are too dark or cold need more "Yin" energy, which the bowl provides.

Moving from Tibet across the land to Celtic regions, here we find a crater. The form of this cup, bowl, or goblet often depended on the means of the bearer. Nonetheless, at least one special cup was present at many gatherings, often passed hand-to-hand around a circle in a show of unity and trust. If carved with special runes, the cup would surely shatter and break should any poison go therein. Beyond this the bowl or drinking horn also represented immortality, as heroes were greeted in the afterlife with a horn filled from the base of the Yggdrasil Tree that when supped, conferred eternal life.

Among the many gods to have special vessels on altars, we look to Poseidon in Greece. Here people used a special stemmed cup for libations called the kantharus and another bowl or wine offerings called the philae. Except during festivals, being drunk was thought of as terribly insulting to the Divine being to whom those offerings went.

Romans had similar customs thanks in part to the Deity Bacchus whose spirit was thought present each time a person served wine!

The writings about a Gallo-Roman goddess, Flora, spoke of the chalice that flowed with milk and nourished the city. Here we find a strong parallel with Lakshmi except now the milk is soma, a drink served in special cups. Only a select few people were entrusted with the task of preparing this beverage.

The symbolic parallels don't end there. If we look at the medieval stories of the Holy Grail, Christ's blood moved into the heart of this "womb" when he sacrificed himself. While Christ is masculine, the cup becomes his womb (the principle of life). In this manner and others, the Bible seems to stress the cup as a marker of human destiny, depending on what it holds! Some cups are bitter (Matthew 26:39), and others overflow with blessings (Psalm 23:5).

The Grail in particular held the seeds of a tradition, but that seed needs to be planted in our soul to grow! I find it interesting that Muslim saints enjoy a cup of love or the wine of gladness in paradise. Zen mystical writings on cups likewise link them with the heart, sensitivity, and intuition, talking about how our illumination begins inside when the practitioner focuses his or her spiritual concentration (plants the seed in that womb). We find enlightenment—enLIFEenment when we reconnect with the Sacred Self.

Perhaps it is for this reason that drinking from one cup is a common practice in weddings. From China to Europe, placing one cup to a couple's lips sealed the vow and entwined two souls into a new wholeness. Japanese couples exchange cups to represent faithfulness.

Buying or Making?

In a brief survey of practitioners I know, most people purchased their bowls and cups because there's such a great variety available in the market at good prices. And unless you're gifted with clay work or carving, that's likely the best choice. Bear in mind that only certain types of clay and wood finishes are suitable for using with edibles or beverages.

Before you shop, think briefly of the function (or functions) for which this tool is intended. Choose the size, shape, medium, and color accordingly. I have found some of the most amazing bowls and cups at secondhand outlets and flea markets, bearing all types of magickal imagery including hexes and god and goddesses (all less than $5!). Also consider checking this Pagan auction site that frequently features all kinds of affordable tools and supplies: *www.pagantradingpost.com/lcgi-bin/auction.pl*

Divination in a Cup

It's easy to see how cups could be used in ritual to hold a beverage for sharing or libations. It's also easy to see how one might find a decorative bowl for herbs and spell components and keep it set aside for special, magickal moments. But what about other uses for these implements?

Divination employing bowls or bowl-shaped dishes is traditionally called lecanomancy. In Babylon, a diviner would pour water, water, and oil, or water and flour into a specially designated bowl. The reader then would watch the behavior of the liquid for divine information. For example, if the querent were asking about a war and the liquid and oil split, that meant divided loyalties. Or if flour  formed in the shape of a lion on the East side of the bowl, that meant a strong spirit would be either aiding or hurting the cause in that direction.

An alternative to this approach requires three bowls filled with three different liquids. Designate one bowl as positive, one bowl as negative, and one as uncertain outcomes. Close your eyes and think of a question. When it's clear in your mind, open your eyes and the bowl in which the liquid is rippling or moving clockwise indicates your answer. Note: this works best for very simple questions unless you want to scry the surface of that liquid afterward for more images. If you're planning to continue the divination by scrying, I suggest dropping food coloring into each bowl before asking your question (such as black for negative, green for positive, and red for neutral). This makes it easier to get results.

A slightly different type of divination begins with a copper bowl. It's called chalcomancy. Historians believe this may have originated in Tibet where the bowl would be rung, then the sound itself was interpreted for meaning based on clarity, evenness, etc. You can often get small brass or copper meditation bowls for this purpose at New Age shops and Eastern gift stores.

Divination using cups or glasses and vases is called scyphomancy. The Greeks and Romans highly ritualized this practice. After three days of calm weather, the diviner dressed in white. He or she prepared a silver cup with wine, a copper cup with oil, and a glass cup filled with water. The querent then posed a question. Movements or images observed in the silver cup spoke of the past, those in the copper cup spoke of the present, and those in the glass were of the future. If only one cup held images, it was felt that it revealed the time frame most important to the question. This particular method compares with the one for bowls previously mentioned, and if you don't have three types of glasses, you could color the water symbolically instead.

In Japan and Trinidad, healers looked to cups for the outcome of cures. In Japan if a patient's medicine cup gets overturned, it's an omen of fast recovery. Similarly, a Trinidad lookman (healer) places a cup filled with water on a patient's head and inquires about the patient's soul. Should the water spill out, it's a positive omen.

Special cups and bowls are often used for tassomancy (tea leaf reading) and for scrying liquids. In the case of tea leaf reading, I suggest a white or light-colored cup so that you can see residual patterns clearly. Put a little dry, loose tea in the cup, add hot water, and swirl the cup three times clockwise while thinking of your question. Now carefully drain off the liquid. Turn the cup over, tap once, then turn it right-side up. Look at the remnant leaves for patterns as you might an inkblot.

If using a bowl for scrying liquids, I've often found a dark bottom works better (and sometimes I float glitter or an opalescent soap (such as Ivory Liquid Soap) on the surface. For people new to scrying, having something to catch your eye makes your efforts more successful. Think about your question and just relax. Try not to look directly at the bowl, but to a point inside just beyond the liquid's surface. Start by trying for about five minutes and then slowly increase the time until you notice movement or images appearing. Make notes of your experiences.

To interpret your reading, first go with what makes sense to you. A heart image, for example, likely has something to do with relationships. Is it whole, separating, coming together? If all you're seeing is movement in the water, typically clockwise and upward mean positive (or a yes), counter-clockwise and downward are negative (or no).

Chapter 10

Brooms and Besoms

There should be less talk; a preaching point is not a meeting point. What do you do then? Take a broom and clean someone's house. That says enough.

—Mother Teresa

The word *broom* comes from the Old English term *besma*, meaning bundle of twigs. In German it was *besmon*, French, *besma*, and Dutch *bezem*. It is no coincidence that all these words resemble our Wiccan term besom. Magickally speaking, brooms are used in a wide variety of spells and rituals, including those for cleansing, luck, and weather (typically calling the rain).

History

Up until the late 1700s brooms were made by hand. Sometimes they were made from tree branches, straw, hay, or corn husks. Other times the herb *Cytisus scoparius* was used (also used for basket weaving), and crude brooms were designed by adding these base elements to a handle (stick). Flax twine attached the two parts, but the end result didn't last very long when applied to the rough floors of caves, cabins, and castles. It also didn't work very well when faced with the remnants of wood and ashes for the hearth fire, no matter how determined the housewife. In fact, the phrase "flying off the handle" came about from when a mother would shoo children outside to play using a stern word and sweep of her broom. As she did, bits of the broom often went flying!

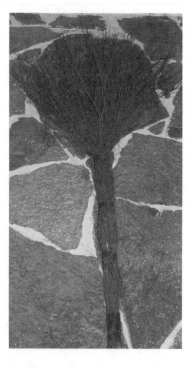

European brooms were similar. The task of making brooms took place in south England where birch grows readily (the predominant wood for handles). The people entrusted with this task were called Besom Squires, who often employed assistants to work on individual brooms. Two other popular trees used for broom handles were ash and hazel. I find it interesting that all three of these trees still have connections with Witchcraft.

The first change in the broom came when a clever farmer named Levi Dickenson determined to make a new type of broom for his wife. He used tassles from sorghum grain. These were more durable, but still fell apart. This set Levi to thinking about a machine that could help him make better brooms. By 1810 the foot-treadle broom machine had been invented and helped spur the industrial revolution! This new broom had pegged handles and bracing. And thus we come to another great saying's origin—"square peg in a round hole." How? Well, the broom makers drilled round holes in the handle but didn't have round pegs. They had to try and split square pegs instead (if the peg wasn't done correctly, it either wouldn't fit or would fall out!). By the mid 1800s, more than 60,000 brooms were being produced annually.

As an odd note, it was also during the 1800s that women performed what was called a broom drill to raise funds for the needy. Eight, 16, or 32 young women comprised each drill team and learned a drill similar to those of military men using guns. Men bought admission tickets to watch the performance, and at the end many a bachelor bought the women's brooms for a good price (all for the greater good, of course!).

Sweeping Superstition

As with so many other beloved household items, the broom has a plentiful body of folk-beliefs associated with it, some of which we can apply to our magickal practices if we so choose. These include:

- ๑ Placing a broom near your doorway represents a wedding in Welsh tradition. Note that a broom is often part of modern Wiccan handfasting rites. By the way, divorce was much easier then—you just had to jump backwards over the same broom with your soon-to-be ex!

- ๑ If a couple wishes to conceive, they should jump a broom together (this is still sometimes used in fertility spells).

- ๑ To protect your home from malevolent sorcerers, place your broom across the threshold (Wales).

In other regions, this action keeps bad luck at bay, especially if enacted on New Years.

❧ To keep your lover true, sweep a circle around him or her (United States).

❧ Sweep your house from the outside in to keep good fortune where it belongs. On the other hand, if you've had bad luck, sweep it from the center outward. This might be adapted to read clockwise and counterclockwise, respectively, in order to add a metaphysical twist.

By far the most popular bit of lore regarding the broom is that Witches rode upon them at Sabbat. Of course, such is the whispering of an uninformed and often fearful mind. In reality, the jumping and running with the broom was a kind of rite for abundance, specifically to make the crops grow as high as they could jump.

Making a Simple Broom

Begin by finding a branch from a fallen tree, preferably about 1 inch in diameter. The length is up to you (an altar-top broom can be quite small, while one used to mark your Circle should be kitchen size).

To get rid of the bark you can either shave it with a drawing knife, or soak it for several days in water (after which most of the bark flakes off). At this point, I suggest sanding the broom handle, first using coarse grade paper, then slowly going to a finer grade. Afterward you can use a stain and/or sealant to help keep you from getting any splinters when you use this tool; otherwise, you'll need to oil the wood regularly to keep it from cracking. The oiling process has the extra advantage that you can (a) make the oil yourself using personally significant herbs and (b) it puts more of your energy into the tool.

Next you need to find what you want to attach for the broom portion. I grow both heather and broom, and like to use a combination of the two dried with their flowers still in place. While the flowers will inevitably fall off, it's usually during a spell or ritual and makes for a lovely strewn effect.

Cut long pieces of whatever you've chosen (for visual effect, no shorter than one third the size of the broom handle). Take these, along with good, strong twine, and begin the process of connection. First lay out a long piece of twine in both directions under the broom handle on the floor (you may actually find that using several pieces is easier than risking tangles). Either configuration allows a more decorative criss-cross pattern over the plant pieces.

Now, take small gatherings of plant fiber starting at the front of the broom so that one third to one half of the fiber is hanging over the edge of the handle. Hold the first bundle of fiber in place with one hand, and wrap it down with the other. Knot it. Repeat this clockwise around the broom in four equidistant locations. This is really the hardest part. Keep in mind the Four Elements and Four Quarters as you work, and consider adding a special incantation for these initial fittings.

Repeat this process to fill in the missing areas, four spots at a time clockwise around the handle. Continue adding plant fiber until the broom looks bushy, then tie off the twine securely. Decorate as you wish.

I don't recommend this simple broom for any type of active cleaning, as it's not overly sturdy. However, it works very well to asperge a space, and as a makeshift wand. Smaller altar-top versions also double as a smudge stick should you decide to burn a little of the herbs. (Have water handy to put it out in case the fire gets out of control!)

Spells

There are numerous spells that utilize brooms as a component. Most are very simple and reflect the broom's symbolic value quite well. Here are some examples:

ᛦ To get an unwanted guest to leave, put your broom next to the threshold of the house. This will "sweep" them away. Similarly, if you feel a recent visitor wished you ill, make sure to sweep out the house he or she leaves to keep them from returning, and to move that negativity away from your sacred space.

ᛦ To bring the rain, dip the sweeping end of your broom in water and sprinkle it out on the ground (to show the gods what you wish). To turn away a storm, however, place the broom lengthwise over the doorway (so as to make an extra covering).

ᛦ To safeguard your land, take a new broom and sweep counterclockwise around the land. Focus on your intention to keep away all maliciousness. Take this broom to a crossroads at midnight and leave it there. Do not turn back.

ᛦ To attract a mate, dress your broom in clothing befitting the person of your dreams. Leave this by the front threshold to welcome that energy. Outside, sprinkle rose petals on the walk so that love finds its way to your door. Alternatively, go and dance with your broom beneath a full moon, envisioning your perfect partner.

ᛦ Anytime life is chaotic, sweep the area in front of your house to remove "clutter."

ᛦ Last but not least, hang a broom near your doorway with the brush end up to bring love into the home (channeled from the Earth to the wand part of the broom handle), and scattered by the bristles.

Chapter 11

Candles

*How far that little candle throws his beams! So shines a good
deed in a naughty world.*

—William Shakespeare

It is a generally accepted humorous truism in the Neo-Pagan
community that if you can think of no other gift for a friend, it's
always safe to get candles! They have so many magickal and
mundane uses that one would be hard pressed to have "too
many." From representing the God and Goddess on our altars
to lighting the way for a magickal meal, there is little in life or
spirituality that isn't enhanced by the gentle glow of a candle.

Wax and Wane

As early as the fouth century B.C., people in China and
Japan made candles from seed or insect wax and molded them
using paper tubes. India utilized wax skimmed from cinnamon
for temple tapers. It's the Romans, however, who are credited

with creating a candle wick, to help travelers through the dark (especially those going to temples).

In Europe, tallow, made by rendering animal fat, was a favored candle-making material. Because of its odor, beeswax was preferred, though considered the choice of the elite due to its expense. Meanwhile, across the water, early Native Americans burned candlefish, missionaries in the southwest used Cerio bark to obtain wax, and settlers in New England got it from bay berries. Mind you, it takes 1 1/2 quarts of bayberries to make one 8-inch candle!

Come the 1800s, the whaling industry created a major change in candle making—namely the use of sperm whale oil. The spermaceti wax didn't yield a terrible smell when burned and it was much harder than even beeswax. Shortly thereafter, the contemporary candle-making industry began to take shape. In 1834, Joseph Morgan introduced a molded candle production machine, followed in 1850 by the development of paraffin, which made most other forms of candles obsolete thanks to its inexpensive nature and durability.

While it's not surprising that the invention of the lightbulb in 1879 put a distinct slump in the industry, it didn't take long for candles to bounce back as a decorative item for the home, gift-giving, celebrations, and religion.

Candle Lore

When blown out, birthday candles release the celebrant's wish with the candle's smoke to the winds. It's thought that this custom may have originated either in the use of incense and other perfumes that sent prayers to the gods, or in rites to Artemis (to honor her sacred fire). In the case of the latter, Greeks took round, moon-like cakes to Artemis' temple during the full moon topped with candles to make the cake "glow" like the lunar sphere.

Another possibility is that we adapted the tradition from Germany, where layered cake was part of birthday celebrations. To this they added small candles in the center to represent life's light and ongoing vitality. In either case, there's no question that candles played an important role in wishing superstitions. And that's certainly not all. Here are a few of the beliefs centered around a candle's flame:

- When a candle burns blue it indicates the presence of a ghost (this idea might be adapted as a type of omen and sign reading).

- A candle sparking indicates either a forthcoming argument or an important message.

- A candle that doesn't light or goes out quickly is a bad omen, often of storms (be they natural or emotional).

- A candle that's allowed to burn to the candlestick socket brings misfortune on the home (this may have been more fact than fiction in that burning a candle increased the chance of household fires).

- Lighting a candle with your right hand brings luck.

- Receiving the gift of a bayberry candle on New Years ensures prosperity.

- Light a candle at a child's birth to afford them extra protection in life.

There are many more, but a large number of the superstitions tie directly into divination by candles (which we'll be talking about next).

Magick by Candlelight: Divination, Spells, and Rituals

There are three different forms of divination that center around candles. The first is perhaps the most widely known, namely pyromancy (observances of the candle's flame). Technically speaking, pyromancy can apply to *any* type of flame, but in this case it will refer to a candle.

To begin, I suggest choosing a candle whose color matches the theme of your question (such as red for matters of the heart or passion). Put the candle in a sturdy container on a table. Sit across from it and try to relax. Take a few deep breaths and begin thinking about your question (take care not to breathe heavily toward the candle as this can skew the results).

As you watch the flame, note its color, shape, and overall behavior, then interpret accordingly. Here is a list of a few possible interpretations:

- Bright, clear flames are a positive answer.
- A flame that blazes suddenly speaks of something unanticipated.
- A candle that won't light is a very bad omen (or a "not now" sign).
- If the candle burns only faintly, it's an indication that there are many mitigating factors that cause uncertainty, especially with actions.
- Flickering flames represent a lack of support for your intended course of action.
- A long-burning flame is a good omen.
- A constantly moving flame means the situation is in flux.

- ❧ Predominantly blue flames tell of spirits near by, orange flames reflect warm emotions, red flames warn of anger, and yellow flames speak of the need to communicate clearly.
- ❧ Rings appearing in the flame presage good news.
- ❧ A smoldering flame implies trouble soon to follow.

I should note at this juncture that some people get full images in the flame much as some people see visions in a crystal. However, this is somewhat rare. Scrying is an art that takes a little time and effort to learn, so be patient with yourself. Try for only a few minutes at first, and then slowly increase the time until you achieve success.

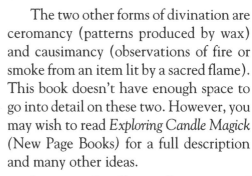

The two other forms of divination are ceromancy (patterns produced by wax) and causimancy (observations of fire or smoke from an item lit by a sacred flame). This book doesn't have enough space to go into detail on these two. However, you may wish to read *Exploring Candle Magick* (New Page Books) for a full description and many other ideas.

In terms of spells, candles are one of the most versatile tools for which the clever and budget-minded Witches could hope. The lighting of a candle can signal the outset of a spell or a desired goal. The blowing out of a candle can release energy (like wishes). And the flame of the candle makes an excellent focus for centering ourselves before magickal workings.

For both spellcraft and rituals, a lot of Wiccans like to dress their candles. Dressing simply means dabbing the candle with a suitable aromatic oil, specifically one whose scent matches the goal of the working. I like to do this from the bottom upward if I'm building energy, and from the top downward if I'm looking for something to decrease or wane.

Speaking of rituals, in this space four elementally colored candles can mark the Four Corners and honor the Watchtower. A single white candle becomes a symbol of the Divine Presence, often being lit when the God and Goddess are invoked. Finally, a candle per person at special rites (especially for unity) shows loving intention and full spiritual commitment at the Circle.

Making Your Own Candles

Almost anyone who has ever gone to summer camp has probably made a milk carton candle (and with milk cartons coming in several sizes now, you have options). However, I'd like to talk about two other forms of candle making that are both relatively fast and easy. The first is rolled candles.

You can get flat pieces of wax at nearly any craft store. You will also need a piece of wick (longer than the wax square), and any herbs or oil you'd like. A hair dryer is also a good helpmate here, as it allows you to warm the wax evenly with very little fuss.

Begin by cutting the wax into the size you'd like the candle to be. For rolling you want the width to be at least twice the length (this improves burning time). Warm the sheet with your hair dryer and lay the wick at one edge with 1 inch hanging out the top (that's what you'll light). Sprinkle any fine herbs or oils inside, warming the wax a little so it accepts either, and then just roll it up! You can heat the final edge a little more if you find it's not holding.

By the way, you can layer your rolled candles so they have more than one color. You need to warm the wax before placing another on top of it. You won't want too many layers or it becomes hard to roll (and you'll have a very fat candle). In any case, you follow the same basic instructions. When you're done rolling and the candle's secure, take a pan that you don't mind keeping for nonedible substances and warm it. Put the bottom of the rolled candle on the heated surface and you instantly have a nice, even bottom!

A second type of easy candle to make is a poured one. You can buy molds for poured candles or just use a sturdy container that you like from around your house (mason jars work very well). Sand, halved orange skins, and even seashells work too.

For the mason jar, begin by knotting your wick and sliding it through a small square of aluminum foil (folded several times for weight). Tie the other end of the wick to a chopstick or pencil and suspend it across the jar so the wick stays in the middle of the container.

Warm your wax. Pour just a little in the bottom of the container and let it cool. This secures the end of the wick firmly in place. Now, slowly pour the rest of the liquid wax inside. Note that you can do this in layers if you wish, but you must wait for each layer to cool completely before adding the next one. I don't recommend self-contained candles much over 6 inches in height, as these tend to burn out more easily.

If you're using a sand, citrus, or other disposable mold, about the only difference is that you'll be removing the candle from its cooling container. If you want small votive-type candles, for example, use an ice-cube tray. You still need to weight each wick (a long stick works for securing the other ends across the length of the tray), but when the wax cools the little candles literally "pop out" without any problem!

Sand candles are also fun. Begin with some play sand that's damp and well compacted. Shape it as you wish. Now take a large serving spoon and hold it in one hand over the sand.

Pour the wax onto that spoon so that it slowly drizzles into the sand mold (this keeps the shape intact). Let this cool for five hours. Finally, heat the candle with a blow dryer from the outside. This adheres just a little of the sand to the candle's surface. The rest you can just knock off.

No matter what type of candles you end up making, please remember to choose the size, shape, color, and aromatics so they match your magickal goals. You can also decorate them with crystals or pressed flowers, and make the candles during astrologically favorable times to improve the overall meaningfulness and results.

Cauldrons

Double, double, toil and trouble
Fire burn, and cauldron bubble.

—William Shakespeare

The word *cauldron* comes from the Latin *caldarium*, meaning hot bath. Previous to this inference, the Middle Irish word was *coire* or *caere*, meaning place of liquid—including those items that have nothing in common with what we picture mentally as a cauldron. In any case, by modern definition, a cauldron is a large metal pot used for cooking over an open fire. To achieve this the cauldron has three legs, and gets attached to a large tripod hanger. Mind you, I have seen cauldrons of other materials modernly, and many Witches prefer their stove top to the open pit fires.

Mythologically speaking, historians and folklorists believe the Holy Grail legends may have ties to the earlier stories of wondrous cauldrons endowed with magickal abilities. Take, for example, the five feasting halls of Irish tradition, each one of which had a cauldron that cooked just the right amount for all in attendance. Or what about Bran the Blessed in Welsh stories? He owned a cauldron of regeneration given to him by a giant. There's also the Celtic Goddess Cerridwen who had a cauldron of inspiration, death, and rebirth. It was from her elixir that the great bard Talisen was fabled to have gotten his talents.

With that in mind, it's not surprising to discover that the Celts used the cauldron to represent abundance, health, creativity, fertility, and rebirth. Interestingly enough, Greek mythology seems to concur on the last point. It says the Goddess of Witches, Medea, could restore people's youth through using a magick cauldron. Sadly, modern cookery has made this item relatively obsolete.

Cookin' Up History

You'd be hard pressed to go into nearly any ancient setting and not find something akin to a cauldron. By far, however, cauldrons held special importance to the Celts, who used them in daily life as well as religion. The early Celtic cauldrons were made of brass and bronze, and were often decorated extensively. The metal alone made cauldrons expensive, meaning only the wealthy could afford them. The additional artistic element helped ensure that sale!

The early cauldrons were either made from one flat sheet, or several sheets riveted together. Where there were several sheets, solder became a connector. In either case, the process was laborious—heating, hammering, soldering, and repeating to ensure a watertight surface.

It wasn't until around 1500 C.E. that iron cauldrons replaced bronze. The best pots of this period had to be a finger thick, and large enough to hold 20 pounds of material (presumably for use at keeps and castles). Where iron pots weren't feasible, earthenware and glass were used, but of course they were far more prone to breakage. Nonetheless, iron wasn't liked by all. Many people thought the iron looked dirty, took too long to heat, and that some of the metal was brittle.

As an interesting side note in the cauldron's history, the Catholic church uses this, too. They have a large cauldron of water into which a lit candle gets plunged repeatedly at Christmas. This is a way of making holy water!

Metaphysical Symbolism and Uses

Cauldrons bear a womb-like shape, which explains their connection with ancient goddesses such as Ceriddwen,

from whose cauldron all inspiration flowed. In magick, we see the three-legged construction of the cauldron as a symbol of the three-fold Feminine Divine (Maiden, Mother, Crone). In this pot, all manner of things might be made from potions and ointments to post-ritual feasts! (Although one would hope that the ointment pot wasn't the same as that for dinner.)

When the cauldron is used in ritual, it's usually placed in the West when bearing liquid or in the South when bearing fire. However, this may change significantly depending on its function. For example, if being utilized for a communal potion, it makes more sense to place the cauldron in the center of the sacred space. It also makes sense to place a fire cauldron in this location if people will be making wishes into it.

At Samhain/Hallows another use for the cauldron is scrying. Traditionally, we believe the veil between worlds grows thin at this time of year, making otherworldly information and communications easier. In particular, a trained medium can use this as a gateway for welcoming and honoring ancestral spirits, which is suited to a festival of the dead. I personally find it difficult to scry plain liquid. If you find you have similar troubles, try sprinkling the surface of your cauldron with some blessed fairy dust (fine glitter) or swirl in a small cup of ivory-colored dish liquid. Both mediums seem to improve results.

Seasonally, consider decorating your cauldron with fruits and flowers to honor the Wheel of Time. Or use your cauldron as a substitute for the sacred fire, and jump over it during rituals for change (this comes in very handy if you live in an area that experiences regular fire bans). The transition from one side of the cauldron to the other represents some type of transmutation— past to the future, bad habit being released, changing bad luck, inspiring fertility, and so on. For safety reasons, I highly recommend keeping the cauldron for this purpose on the small side (knee height and not too wide).

For this Kitchen Witch, perhaps my favorite function for the cauldron is in making proverbial "stone soup" at a festival. This is where people from several camps come together with what they can share and literally mix and mingle the blend to perfection. You never know how the soup will taste, but you can always be assured of some good fellowship.

Making or Buying Your Cauldron

Making a functional cauldron that will withstand cooking heats is very difficult in most modern Witches homes (unless you have a forge handy). So, just for the fun of it I went to Froogle and checked. You can get all manner of cauldrons—ones that have lights, ones that give off smoke and fog, and ones made from a wide variety of mediums for less than $30 (depending on how elaborate you want to get). The best buys, including altar-sized iron cauldrons, seem to come from Halloween supply shops (hey, let's hear it for commercialization!). EBay proved to be another great resource, even stocking small silver cauldron charms (great gifts) for less than $5. If you're not online, check secondhand shops and any place that specializes in costumes, rentals, and supplies.

Now, if you don't mind making a temporary cauldron that won't withstand external fire, but is fun for Halloween and Fall Festivals, you can start with a handy pumpkin. Open this up and scoop it out like you would for a Jack-o-Lantern. About 1 inch in from the rim, cut a decorative pattern into the meat (making sure to save three equalsized triangles, which will become your cauldron's feet). Now, slice into the bottom of your pumpkin in three places equally spaced on the bottom. Slowly widen them until they'll accept the triangles of meat so you have your "feet." Fill the pumpkin with aluminum foil on the inside edge so you can use it to dispense candy at the ritual.

Chapter 13

Costumes

The same costume will be Indecent 10 years before its time, Shameless 5 years before its time, Outré (daring) 1 year before its time, Smart, Dowdy 1 year after its time, Hideous 10 years after its time, Ridiculous 20 years after its time, Amusing 30 years after its time, Quaint 50 years after its time, Charming 70 years after its time, Romantic 100 years after its time, Beautiful 150 years after its time.

—James Laver

The Mask is used at those times when human experience is transforming—birth, death, initiation, seasons of the year—the basic cycle of life.

—John Mack, *Masks and the Art of Expression*

When you think of a costume, what comes immediately to mind? Is it the image of the Lone Ranger, or perhaps children donning regalia on Halloween to portray an alternate persona? Is it the superhero of your youth who used costumes and a mask to safeguard his or her identity? Or what about our modern costumes? Doctors and dentists have specialized clothing, as do actors who apply costumes and masks to develop believable characters for their audience. Today, each of these seems perfectly fitting in their setting, yet they whisper relentlessly of a faraway time and mysterious customs.

All Decked Out

Mask-wearing and religious costuming is a tradition with roots delving well into the distant past of our species. The ancient Egyptians, for example, had gold funerary masks that communicated Divine power and thereby gave the spirit status in the afterlife. Other similar masks were found at Incan and Aztec burial sites. Shamans used costumes regularly in ritual, and primitive peoples in a wide variety of global settings wore masks and other decorative items to appease the spirits of Nature. You'd actually be hard pressed to find any early religion that did not have some special manner of dressing (either daily or for special rites) detailed out for either the priests or adherents.

So what exactly is it about costume that has kept it part of the human condition for such a long time? The answer to this question is multifaceted. First, costumes help us investigate the depths of our imagination. Here, for a few moments we can retreat from "normalcy" and explore limitless possibilities, quite literally walking a mile in different shoes. From this vantage point we gain unique perspectives into animals, plants, and personas. In fact, this was exactly the effect many medicine men and wise people hoped to achieve.

Once behind the layers of a costume, you were no longer recognizable to other villagers but literally became the face of folk heroes, helpful spirits, and even Deities. For example, some medicine men in Africa wore masks designed to represent the face of an appropriate spirit when effecting cures. The hope was to better relate to that force, become possessed, and thereby produce miracles. From the patient's perspective this must have been a formidable sight!

Costumes and masks tap into a primitive side of our nature, expressing fears and hopes in allegorical form. It is this very form that found its way into magick and religious observance. Beginning with paintings left by cave dwellers, we see that adornment participated readily in imitative magick. As part of the sacred dances to ensure a productive hunt, people readied costumes of the desired beast. They then enacted a mime of sorts where the person embodying the creature got captured. This magickal parody represented the tribe's ambition as an accomplished feat. The idea was to metaphysically affect the creature as portrayed, and therefore have a successful expedition.

In this illustration, the costume fulfills several important functions religiously and socially. First, it provides the symbolism necessary to empower the magickal rite. Second, it visually gives the participants something positive to focus on. Third, it becomes a central figure to rally around, inspiring the hunters before they begin their tasks. Finally, it honored the spirit of the beast being hunted.

A small sampling of costumes and masks from the Royal Ontario Museum and The Metropolitan Museum of Art reveal those intended for the harvest, healing, death, sickness, and all the major events marking human existence. And knowingly or not, even modern-minded folk aren't without their social costume, office costume, and yes—ritual costume! Each one has a purpose, a role on the stage of life; each guise is but one facet of the greater individual.

Costume Craft

In looking at our community, it's obvious that we utilize costumes regularly. Be it a ritual robe, a Green Man mask, personally meaningful jewelry, or a lovely display of glitter somewhere on our bodies, we are doing much as our ancestors did—express a goal or purpose through what we wear and how we wear it.

Costumes need not be fancy to evoke all the energies you desire. Sometimes just wearing something different and special when enacting a spell or ritual gives you that extra boost. For example, I find it awkward to do the ritual Fire dance when I'm in jeans, but don a flowing skirt, and suddenly my mood and perspective changes. The way a skirt flows and moves with the rhythm, my body, and whatever energy is being created "feels" right. That simple little cue helps frame my mind more toward spirituality and magick.

As with other tools, you'll need to do some test driving to see what type of costumes help you similarly (in specific metaphysical situations). Besides wanting the outfit to help improve your focus for the working, it should also somehow reflect the theme of the spell or ritual. Thanks to a wide variety of fabrics these days, you may be able to reflect that theme through your chosen outfit color, fabric pattern, or texture. You can also create some pretty amazing effects with very little money.

For example, if you're looking for comfort, wear comfortable clothes that have that cuddly appeal. One option would be wrapping yourself in a flannel blanket at the part of the spell where you're invoking that sense of reassurance. In this case, the blanket is both a costume and a component that you will wear for the rest of the time you are working, and that illustrates your goal.

112

A second example would be that of a dramatic cloak for ritual theater that doesn't take a lot of time or money. In this case, get some inexpensive remnant fabric, cover it with spray fabric glue, and sprinkle on whatever color glitter you want! It will look awesome in firelight—no need for sewing unless you're feeling picky! Remember that in the dark you can get away with creating illusions as opposed to needing highly detailed costumes.

Because there are literally hundreds of types of costumes you may want to make for yourself, I'd like to describe two very simple items that can be adapted to a wide variety of goals.

Basic T-Tunic

Note that by extending the lines of the T-tunic to fit your height you can make a Celtic-looking ritual robe!

Begin with 3 yards of fabric that is at least 45 inches wide (this will fit an average-sized or medium build person). Fold the fabric in half from top to bottom and lay the fabric flat. Next, take one of your long-sleeved shirts that buttons down the front and put it on. Open the buttons until you can easily pull this shirt off over your head. Now lay this shirt in the middle of the fabric with the sleeves straight out to each side. Cut 3 inches out from this "pattern" on each side (you're basically cutting out two rectangles, one on the left side and one on the right—we'll worry about the top in a minute).

Fold the fabric in half as it lays from left to right. Make a tiny snip along the fold. This is the point from which you'll be cutting a half circle for your head. Use the point of your button-down shirt to eye how big you want the opening to be (bearing in mind you'll be folding under this neckline to keep the fabric from fraying).

113

Before doing any sewing, this is the point at which it's easiest to add trim to the sleeve or bottom if you wish. You can lay it out in several places and see where you want it (if at all). Pin and stitch this before doing seams (take care that the trim is measured so it lays in the same place on both sides, otherwise it will be obviously uneven after putting in the seams).

I find it's easier to pin the neckline (folded under half an inch twice from the outside inward) before the sides are completed. If you want to cheat a little, you could just use a finished piece of trim and iron it in half. Place the neckline into the middle of the trim, fold, and stitch in place!

Finally, turn the tunic's fabric so the right sides are together. Beginning at the wrist, pin and sew inward and downward 1 inch from the outer edge on both sides. Stop about 3 inches from the bottom of the tunic. This part still needs to be turned under separately and stitched, which allows for a side slit to improve mobility.

Dress up your tunic with a nice belt, a pouch for your ritual tools, or whatever!

Basic Mask

I love cardboard. It's such a wonderfully multi-purpose material. A basic mask begins with a flexible piece of cardboard (one you can bend gently). You also want to assemble paints, glue, feathers, leaves, fur tufts, fabric, scissors, string or elastic, glitter, and other decorative touches that mirror your goal. Obviously, exactly what goes on your mask depends heavily on what it represents. For example, if you're making a Winter King or Queen mask, you might want to use white paint or fabric combined with opalescent glitter and tiny cut outs of snowflakes.

Step two is to cut out a piece of the cardboard that's easily as wide as your face. How large from top to bottom is up to you (and your concept), but I've found they stay in place better when they measure no more than 6 inches. Now, shape your mask, checking to see where the eye holes need to be and how large to cut them. If you have bad eyesight, I suggest a little larger opening for comfort or to allow space for your glasses.

Remember that you need not be exact in your details—you're simply intimating a certain type of energy. A Sun mask, for example, might have sharp triangular edges all the way around (an upward pointing triangle represents Fire, and its an easy shape to cut). Apply color and texture over that base. If painting the surface and/or adding small decorative touches, you may wish to add a clear sealant as a last layer to make sure no paint, glitter, etc. accidentally falls off (which could also land in your eyes or mouth).

Finally, put small holes at the top and bottom of the mask. Run your string or elastic through here, leaving enough so that it fits securely around the back of your head. This final form of the mask won't be an overly durable item, but if cared for, a mask can easily last through several rituals.

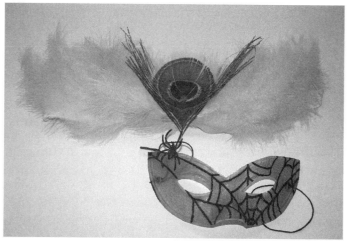

Chapter 14

Crystals

And every sea-god pays a gem,
Yearly out of his watery cell,
To deck great Neptune's diadem.

—Thomas Campion

It has often been a matter of light-hearted jest to say that a Witch without jewelry is basically naked. In looking at our community, there's no doubt that we love our "pretty, shiny things" not only in jewelry but as implements of the altar, components to spellcraft, gardening helpmates, and decorative items in our homes. In that sense of awe and treasure, we're not alone. Humankind has always been drawn to stones and utilized them in a wide variety of ways.

Gem of an Idea

From the earliest recorded history until well into the Middle Ages, acquiring gems had nothing to do with their beauty, and sometimes not even their value. Rather, these things were an important part of daily life, and items that conferred power to those that bore them.

We can look to India and Babylonia as examples. In both area humans considered gems and crystals as magickal—filled with all manner of virtues and energies that could be tapped. The beliefs surrounding stones were quite complex, even to the point of becoming a science (just look to alchemy for verification of this truth later in history).

So valued were these stones that the royal houses would usually consult an astrologer or sage to advise them on what to buy before visiting a jeweler. When people realized that after purchase these gems became central to numerous rituals, including those for healing and spiritual attunement, it's no wonder that no expense or consultation was spared. The Vedas (scriptures of Indian culture) even went so far as to assign nine gems to various birth times, laying the groundwork for what would become our Western birthstone customs.

When Arabs came through the Roman Empire in the seventh century, they learned the attributes for the crystals they found and took them back to the Middle East. This, in turn, was refined and came back to Europe with the Crusaders. In fact, the practice of putting a stone at the tip of a magick wand originates with the fairy godmother of some Arabic tales! In this manner, several cultures contributed to the repository of gem lore being shared even among common folk. By the Middle Ages, stones were being used in all kinds of folk magick from protective charms, to bringing sleep, and even as part of healthful potions.

Books on the subject imply that each stone's power was determined in part by its shape or color. A red or heart-shaped stone, for example, was thought helpful to matters of the heart or blood conditions. Similarly, yellow stones might be employed as part of a treatment for jaundice (with accompanying prayers or incantations), and an eye agate would be utilized to "turn" the evil eye away from someone experiencing bad luck. Come the Age of Reason, however, many of these superstitions became somewhat antiquated, and for a while our attention turned more to the value and beauty of a stone than its metaphysical affiliations.

The New Age movement certainly renewed that missing part of the equation, especially toward more readily available (and affordable) crystals. This renewal has also been helped by science, which showed us crystals such as quartz can, indeed, house energy. Modern practitioners utilize a huge variety of stones in an equal variety of ways. The two most common, however, are divination and magickal workings.

Crystal Clear: Divination With Gems and Stones

Divination using crystals, gems, or stones takes the official name of crystallomancy. There are at least two common methods. The first is using the surface of a crystal (often a sphere) as a scrying plane. St. Augustus thought that crystallomancy began in Persia with beryl spheres. We also know from various writings that it was popular among the Romans who used a variety of polished stone surfaces.

By the fifth century C.E. texts provided an array of instructions for scrying, including those that recommended aquamarine, quartz, and obsidian crystal. The popularity of this art grew and was even embraced by great mines such as Swiss alchemist Paracelsus (1400s) who called scrying "observing rightly."

Along with various bits of advice, mages ritualized the process of crystal scrying by adding cleansings, timing, fasting, invocations, specially prepared stands in which the crystal would sit, and so forth. While part of me respects such an enterprising spirit, another part wants to say, "But it's only a rock!"

119

Crystal experts in the Yucatan would say it wasn't. In this part of the world there were specially trained people who used crystals (as clear as possible), typically to find lost items. In a completely different part of the world, Apache medicine men did something similar, applying crystals to help discern the whereabouts of stolen property.

Crystal gazing is still enjoyed by many practitioners today. The size and type of crystal is really up to you, but I do recommend shopping around, as these pretty stones can get very costly. Most people find a minimum of a 3-inch diameter surface the most comfortable on the eyes.

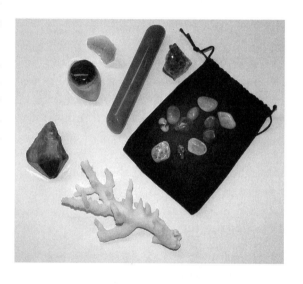

As with candle gazing, you want to put the crystal in a stand on or near eye-height across from you on a table. Relax and breathe very deeply. Think about your question. Don't look exactly at the stone, but at a point somewhere inside or beyond it. Let your vision blur. Watch for clouds or light to form and move (or sometimes full images). That's where the interpretive value begins.

If you are fortunate and get full images, write them down. Use your first impressions and dream guides to sort those out. Otherwise, most often light or clouds that move up and right are a yes or positive response. Light or clouds moving down and left are a negative, or no response. Swirling for more than five minutes is usually the indication that no conclusive answer is available right now. Additionally pay attention to colors, such as blue and green for happiness or good news, and yellow ones for surprises or news.

As a side note, I'd like to mention that some people get other sensual input by focusing on a crystal. They might feel textures, or smell aromas for example. Don't let that dissuade you. Your mind is simply responding to the sense to which it most strongly relates and give you information through it. Write down your experience and think about it. An itchy texture, for example, would be cautionary, while something soft is far more comforting and welcoming.

The second version of crystal divination is creating a set of casting stones of your own choosing. This is my personally preferred system of divination, so I'll tell you how I went about it (and you can tinker from there). First, I pondered the casting surface. The available material was a Victorian napkin with lace embroidery. I decided that the lace area would be South, the center of the napkin would represent present/personal information, and the Four Corners would be Elemental, and the edges the future. Again, there is no reason to use my construct, but it often helps to have ideas from which to start figuring out your own system.

Next is determining how many stones you want in your grouping. I chose 13 for the 13 moons. Each stone's meaning in this configuration comes from its lore, color, and metaphysical meaning, coupled with where it lands in a casting. For example, an eye agate that lands in the East would imply the need to be watchful of communication (eye agates were protective, and East is the Air element—that is, communications).

I think you can easily see where detailing out a system such as this is impossible in such a short space. You have a lot of options both in mediums and surfaces. However, I do strongly suggest carefully choosing stones that have similar sizes, and that seem to mingle well together. Just as a Tarot deck, this is a cooperative venture. Over the years, some new stones have come to me (I find them or get them as gifts); other stones leave, but always there's a harmony and balance in the mix. If you achieve this, you're right on target.

Stone Spellcraft and Ritual Applications

It's obvious that the flexibility of crystals doesn't end with divination. As spell components, you can't beat the durability, color, and variety of crystals. Most practitioners use a variety of systems for choosing specific crystals for workings. These include observation of the crystal's color, shape, personal intuition about the stone's energies, and a review of the metaphysical associations for the stone. I would be remiss not to mention that we generally include "metals" in our list of stones, and use those similarly.

Here's a brief list of some stones and metals and their associations:

Crystals

- ꙮ Agate: protective; often used as amulets
- ꙮ Amber: solar/fire symbolism; often use in healing magick
- ꙮ Amethyst: peace, self-control, bravery
- ꙮ Apache tears: luck
- ꙮ Azurite: dream magick and overall accord

- Beryl: improving relationships, legal victory
- Bloodstone: wishes, weather magick
- Calcite: improved concentration, self-healing
- Carnelian: communication skills
- Citrine: banishing bad dreams
- Flourite: improving mental skills and alertness
- Lapis: augmenting psychic abilities
- Moonstone: lunar/water associations
- Plain stones: grounding and centering
- Quartz: multi-purpose magick stone
- Turquoise: travel and weather magick

Metal

- Brass: prosperity and fire magick
- Copper: conducting/moving energy
- Feldspar: fairy magick
- Gold: solar associations—strength, leadership
- Iron: vitality, strength, and protective magick
- Lead: turning malicious magick away from you (banishing)
- Lodestone: attracting energy
- Silver: Goddess energy, inspiration, insightfulness
- Tin: good fortune

I think you can see pretty quickly that there are an abundance of spells to which various crystals could be applied effectively. Generally, however, most Witches seem to use them for charms, talismans, and amulets.

In the ritual space, stones can be one way of honoring a Deity. For example, if you follow Ra, you might place a sunstone (or other gold, red, or yellow stone) on your central altar to represent that energy. Alternatively, you could use crystals to augment the energies of the Elements and Watchtowers by placing stones at East, South, West, and North. Each stone should metaphysically correspond to the Element in which it's placed (such as a blue or purple stone in the West for Water).

Chapter 15

Decorations

Let the realist not mind appearances. Let him delegate to others the costly courtesies and decorations of social life.

—Ralph Waldo Emerson

Just as it's said that "clothes make the man," decorations make the sacred space something truly special. We talked earlier in this book about the psychological advantage to costumes. Decorations have a similar effect. Adornment, especially when used for specific occasions repeatedly, becomes part of tradition and custom. Those traditions and customs shape our thoughts and help us immediately connect with what's happening.

Take the Yule tree as an example. While there were times in history that using evergreen clippings was rather controversial (thanks to the Pagan roots of Christmas in Saturnalia), there is no question that when you see a decorated evergreen you think of Winter Solstice. That mental connection, in turn, improves your ability to make magick based on the theme of the holiday. Sound too simple? Think about it for a minute. How do you feel when you walk into a room filled with balloons and streamers? I'm usually happy and think, party time! While this is a mundane example, it gives you a feel for how decorations can support your magick.

Now, obviously what you use depends heavily on the occasion or working. A birthday circle might well have those balloons and streamers, along with cake afterwards, for example. If the birthday happens to correspond with a rite of passage into adulthood, pictures of the child at younger ages can adorn one side of the room, while gifts symbolizing his or her new adult role await him or her on the other. In this manner, everything within the magickal sphere has a specific meaning that empowers the rite. These props improve the enjoyment of all participants because they reflect the emotions, desires, and general atmosphere befitting that occasion.

As with costumes, your efforts need not be elaborate or expensive to be very effective! Let's consider some specific ideas.

The Seasons

The Wiccan celebration cycle focuses on the Wheel of Time, and specifically the Sun's position in the sky. As we move through the seasons, the decorations in and around our sacred space might aptly reflect the changes in the Earth. In spring, and especially for Beltane, I like to bring early blooming wildflowers into the Circle and cast them around clockwise while calling the Quarters. This is a very small decorative element, but the visual effect is quite lovely. Releasing the petals in this manner also honors the Air element, which is likewise associated with spring. Additionally, if you're working indoors during the day, hang very light or sheer curtains, or none at all so the fullness of spring sunshine can enter your space. Other nice touches for spring include:

- ۞ wind chimes
- ۞ kites (which, in turn, could become part of the ritual or spell for that occasion)
- ۞ images of baby animals (this is when many wild creatures give birth)
- ۞ feathers or fans (paper or electric)

Come summer, consider putting fresh fruits and cultivated flowers around the space in their proper Elemental placement. Hang brightly colored curtains at the entryway, especially those in red, yellow, orange, and gold to honor the Sun. Have some type of fire present in the Circle (in a safe container, so nothing catches on fire). There are some stores that sell electric fire simulators if real fire isn't practicable.

Summer is a high-energy season, the earth is abundant, and these kinds of touches reflect that overall premise.

Fall offers a plethora of color and options. Wax leaves for strewing around the space and the altar. Bring in pumpkins carved with various runes or magickal sigils. Add gourds or Halloween trappings (dry ice is particularly fun and creates a wonderful dramatic effect). This is the perfect time to dust off that cauldron, set up ancestral altars, and rejoice in the harvest.

Finally, winter brings us full-circle. Hues are darker. Black and white is perfectly apt. Make paper snowflakes and dust them with opalescent glitter. Take fallen pine branches and use them on the altar. Stones or living plants might be added to the sacred space to celebrate the Earth element, even as the plant sleeps. Use plenty of candles, bringing light to the darkness and giving strength to the Sun.

As an aside, there are several books on the market regarding ritual that include ideas for decorations. One you might like to check out is my *Wiccan Book of Ceremonies and Rituals* (Kensington/Citadel, 1998).

Other Celebrations and Rituals

Many celebrations and rituals focus on a person, persons, or a group with a specific occasion in mind. In this instance, the desires of the individuals participating in an event should be of primary concern when we choose decorations. This is especially true for deeply personal moments such as eldership, marriage, and Wiccaning rituals. For these celebrations, the dominant choice of emblems becomes the foundation to all your scenery.

To provide an example, a new mother wanted to have a ritual to welcome her baby into the world and thank the God and Goddess for the baby's health. Many of us had already birthed one or more children, so we had all manner of baby items with which to fill the sacred space (some of which were gifts). We also found images of Divine beings who have been regarded as the guardians of mothers and children (Kwan Yin comes to mind as one possibility) and allowed the mother to choose one to whom the ritual would be directed. The cauldron that day was filled with milk, the music that surrounded was Kenny Loggins's "House at Pooh Corner" and other lullabies, and the altar cloth was a light-weight baby blanket. The result was charming, perfectly apt, but not overly time consuming or expensive to produce. Again, the point is not so much doing a lot, but rather having real meaning in the decorations you choose. Unless the ritual is a surprise, I suggest meeting with the individuals involved as we did with this mom, and getting their ideas and feedback. This allows you to begin with a meaningful foundation to which you can bring your creativity, and a lot of times what you need will already be in your home or your friend's home.

Don't overlook little things, including the way you dress, to the colors of various items you bring into the sacred space. Because you are in this "play," you too become a kind of scenery!

As for color, psychology has shown that specific pigments contribute to distinctly different frames of mind. Because of this, minute accents of color amplify the magick at hand. Returning to our birthday party, this means bright, festive colors, especially red, to celebrate life's continuance.

Representative pigments can be part of flower arrangements and any number of other adornments including altar cloths, draperies, lighting (colored lightbulbs), candles, and so on. Here is a brief list of traditional color associations:

Colors

- Red: Life's energy, the element of Fire, vigor, courage, power, zeal, and vitality
- Orange: Sympathy, cordial feelings, growing energy, fruitfulness, kinship, and the harvest
- Yellow: Creativity, fertility, Element of Air, oracular attempts, and whimsy
- Green: Healing, beliefs and convictions, financial matters, and progress or growth.
- Blue: Harmony, rest, the Water Element, happiness, the contemplative nature, and unity
- Purple: Metaphysical topics, the soul, dedication, insight of the higher self, and wisdom
- White: Peace, safety, cleansing, purity, and truce
- Black: Turning negativity, repose, and the unknown
- Brown: Nature, grounding and foundations, and beginnings
- Pink: Friendship, relaxation, improved emotions, moods, and physical well-being

The Witch's tool kit is ready, willing, and able to meet each one of life's special moments with something equally wonderful. Don't be afraid to express your inventive nature when you decorate. The results are well worth the efforts you make, and everyone who participates will appreciate the additional dimension decoration adds to your celebration.

Chapter 16

Divination Tools

The whole world is an omen and a sign. Why look so wistfully in a corner? Man is the Image of God. Why run after a ghost or a dream? The voice of divination resounds everywhere and runs to waste unheard, unregarded, as the mountains echo with the bleatings of cattle.

—Ralph Waldo Emerson

We have discussed a few divination tools specifically in this book, such as mirrors and dowsing implements. Even so, I felt it was worth taking a moment to talk about the function of divination tools in a Kitchen Witch's kit, as well as how one might adapt or create a wholly personal divination system. Unlike other parts of this book, I won't explore the history of such things simply because each divinatory tool's history is unique, and often varies by culture. Suffice it to say, however, that there is little on this planet that someone, somewhere, hasn't tried to use for the purpose of future telling including:

- Alectromancy: observation of sacred roosters as they pick at grain
- Chalcomancy: interpreting the sounds of copper and brass bowls when struck
- Dactylomancy: discerning traits by a person's fingertips and rings
- Gelomancy: reading the meaning in hysterical laughter
- Marcharomancy: divination by knife, sword, or ax
- Oenomancy: prediction based on the appearance and taste of wine
- Transataumancy: readings based on accidentally seen or heard events
- Zoomancy: fortune telling based on sightings of mythical beasts such as the Loch Ness monster

This list certainly gives the modern practitioner an open playing field when considering devising a personalized divination tool. Nonetheless, there are some simple steps you can follow to make the process easier.

1. Foundations: Are you going to base your divinatory system on something that exists, such as making a personal rune set or Tarot deck, or on something completely inspired, such as divination by coupons?

2. Medium: Based on step one, what type of medium do you want to use? If you've chosen the coupon system, you can still make that a little sturdier by putting them on poster board, lamination, or decoupage. If you've chosen another system, think about the longevity of your tool. Once you put forth the effort, you'll probably want this to last a while.

3. Size: How many symbols do you want in your system and what size will each component be? In terms of symbols, I always suggest at least 13 (one for each Moon of the year) as a good starting point. Unless you're making a binary (yes/no) system, this provides you with enough diversity to answer questions a little more clearly.

   As for size, one of the reasons I don't use Tarot a lot is that I find it uncomfortable in my hands (which are small). That discomfort seemed to negatively impact readings until smaller decks came on the market. Eventually, I decided on tumbled stones as my medium because I like their texture and they travel well.

4. Cast, Drawn, Laid Out, or Observed? Most systems lend themselves to one of these four approaches. Once you know which one you prefer, or if you want to integrate more than one, it will help you with the overall design. For example, if you're going to trust your familiar to provide you with omens, you need to set up a list of what movements mean when you're observing him or her. On the other hand, if you're using a set of three-dimensional game pieces, these can be cast or drawn (provided they have a similar enough size not to subconsciously skew the reading). Mixed tumbled stones can be cast, drawn, laid out, and in the case where one seems to take on a life all its own in the reading, also observed.

5. Reversed or Negative Interpretations? Some readers of the Tarot and runes never use reversed meanings. Others do. You need to decide if your system will have a space for these types of energies,

and if so how you will represent them. For example, if I see a "communication" stone land due North of my casting cloth in a reading, to me this means a problem in discourse because North is also the season of winter when things slow down or freeze. It may also represent a waiting period for emotions to figuratively "thaw." How this type of thing translates into your system is up to you, but life is not always rosy, and I do think it a good idea to allow your divination system to communicate those things you may not want to hear but do need to know.

6. Interpretive Values of All Your Symbols? What's what? Right now you need to think about each item in your divination system and determine what it will mean in each reading. Continuity improves the results of your efforts. The more a symbol is used to represent X, the more it attunes to X, and the sooner you relate to it as X without referring to crib notes. I strongly advise writing out your interpretive values and keeping them nearby for several months when you first start testing the system.

7. Trial Runs. Okay, once you're through the first six steps it's time to find a reading buddy with whom to work. Let him or her think of a question, and then cast, draw, lay out, or observe your chosen medium. Make notes of what seems to work, and what needs fine-tuning. Note that most pre-packaged systems take at least three months before a person is wholly comfortable with them. Because you're doing something new, it may take a little longer to see regular success.

In the process of creating your tool, I can promise that your understanding of, and appreciation for, symbolic language increases. This process requires digging deep into your mind (know thyself) to find those symbols to which you respond most strongly, and those that can help you better understand the energies in and around your life. Your divination system is about to become an extension of your magickal life. It will grow even as you do.

Care and Keeping of Your System

Divination tools should receive care and attention. They will pick up random energy when sitting around, and often house residual energies from various readings. Thus I prescribe the following:

1. Blessing
2. Dedication
3. Charging
4. Storage
5. Cleansing and Recharging

Blessing and dedication of your tool takes place after it's created. This invokes the Divine visage of your choice to empower and guide your work. After all, who better to open the windows of understanding and insight? A brief prayer and visualization manages this nicely. Say the words that are on your heart. Indicate how you'll use this implement (for personal use, for others, or both). This second part is your dedication— it's committing the tool to a specific function in your spiritual life.

Charging has been accomplished in a variety of ways, depending on your tradition. Some people leave the tool in the light of the Sun or Moon (I like both to balance the logical and intuitive nature). Others place the tool on their altar for a period of time, or carry/sleep with the tool to attune it to their personal energy. Trust your instincts on this, and remember that your tool may need a refill of energy from time to time.

In terms of storage, I like to have a special place in which to keep my divination tools. My Tarot deck, gifted to me by a wonderful gentleman, stays in a stained-glass box created by Waterhawk Creations. My stones have a satin bag they live in when not in use. This accomplishes two things: I know they're both safe and I also know that they're not being randomly handled or played with, as I have children and pets. The housing for your divinatory tools should be similarly mindful of your lifestyle.

Finally, on a regular basis you may want to cleanse and recharge your implement. Just like a battery, the blessings you placed therein won't last forever, and all the use you give your tool can leave leftovers that aren't helpful to getting sound readings. If you find that your divination system begins to lack the clarity it had previously, try this step and see if it helps. If it doesn't work, it means that you likely need to find or devise something new that reflects the changes and growth you've personally experienced in your spiritual life.

Chapter 17

Dowsing Tools

He will forget it all between the sunset and dawn. It is the three-inch swing of a pendulum in a cupboard, which the great pulse of nature vibrates by and through.

—Henry David Thoreau

Dowsing has been used for thousands of years by diviners, seers, Shamans, and wise people around the world. By employing a forked stick, an L-shaped rod, or an item on a string (such as a ring or pendulum), it's an effective means of psychically discovering various pieces of desired information from the location of a lost item to discovering water wells.

While no one knows exactly how dowsing works, including those who employ it, the theory is that there's some type of energetic connection between the dowser, the tool, and the object that person seeks. All things in this world have an energy signature. By focusing on that goal, the dowser's tool becomes like an antenna that tunes into the seeker's thoughts and the vibrations of the item sought, and refines them both until the item is located.

Some people think that dowsing is just luck, but there have been numerous studies done that indicate this art is far more than happenstance. Great minds, including Leonardo da Vinci, Robert Boyle, and Albert Einstein concur. Einstein in particular held the conviction that a dowsing rod was a tool—and a valuable instrument. He said that this instrument illustrates the way the human nervous system reacts to various unknown outside factors and internal mechanisms, even if we don't completely understand them as yet. Most dowsers agree.

Their Rods Give Them Oracles

The art of dowsing has existed for thousands of years. The implements employed by dowsers varied slightly according to the person and what materials were available. Nonetheless the basic process for dowsing seems relatively unchanged through the millennia.

We begin our exploration of dowsing's rich history in the Tassili Caves of North Africa. Discovered in 1949, the walls of these caves included wonderful pre-historic art. Included in the depictions we find a painting of an unnamed dowser surrounded by his tribe as he sought water. Carbon dating revealed this mural to be more than 8,000 years old.

Egyptian etchings on 4,000-year-old temple walls illustrate the Pharaohs as holding items that historians believe may have been dowsing tools. Tied to this are passages in the Bible that speak of various dowsing, tools such as Aaron's Rod and the Staff of Moses (both of which brought water). The prophet Hozea implies that the Jews learned this technique from the Egyptians when he writes about them consulting pieces of wood or wands.

Records indicate that the Greeks had similar methods by 400 B.C.E. in Crete. One of the methods used by the Oracle at Delphi was that of a pendulum. It's interesting to note that the term rhabdomancy (modernly used for dowsing divinations) came from Homer, a Greek poet. Rhabdomancy translates as divining rod.

Moving forward in history, if we look to Germany during the Middle Ages we find mining tools meant to help uncover ore deposits. Mention of this happens again in the mid-1500s in writings on mining that include the illustration of a dowser. By the 1650s, Martine de Bertereau (a baroness) was traveling with her husband to locate minerals and managed to uncover 150 ore sites in France alone thanks to dowsing. It was during this same period that the English philosopher John Locke wrote about dowsing rods as a means to find both metals and water. Books from the 1700s and 1800s continued to mention dowsing when speaking of these types of efforts. In fact, at the turn of the last century in the United States, a report was given to congress by the U.S. Department of the Interior regarding the feasibility of using dowsing to help find suitable drilling sites.

It's worthy of noting that there are at least 3,500 books about the art of dowsing in the Library of Congress today. About the only notable difference between contemporary tomes on this subject and the ancient treatments is that the applications for dowsing have expanded. People have now begun using dowsing tools to locate archaeological dig sites, discern ley lines (and other types of energy centers), track criminals, locate missing people or pets, in ghost hunting, and so on.

Do It Yourself Dowsing

To try dowsing yourself you must first determine which of the three basic methods you'd like to use.

1. A Forked Stick: the most common type of dowsing rod, this requires finding a Y-shaped tree limb small enough to carry. Many practitioners prefer willow but other woods that have been used for this include peach, dogwood, hazel, mulberry, maple, juniper, and apple. Once you've located a suitable branch, there's no need to get any fancier. Simply hold each side of the Y in your left and right hands, and focus on your goal while walking over a piece of land. When you pass over the right spot, the end of the branch dips downward (this is called a "hit"). Note that this is not always explicitly accurate. It's good to repeat the attempt from various angles to hone in on your goal.

2. Rods: Normally two L-shaped metal or wood rods, one held in each hand parallel to the ground. While you walk the area, you're now watching for the rods to swing widely open, or cross over each other (X marks the spot). In my opinion, a hit is more often discovered at the X, where energy pools (such as a vortex) are shown by the rods opening. Note that you can make a pair of rods for yourself very easily using a heavy duty coat hanger and wire cutters—no fuss!

3. Pendulums: Pendulums can be purchased at a wide variety of stores; however there are other options available to you. For example, if you have a novelty bead that's pointed at one end, you can string that and use the point as the focus of your efforts. I've also had success using an herb bundle, a wedding ring, Austrian crystals (that normally get hung in windows as sun catchers), sewing needles, and so on.

Hints for Making Your Own Pendulum

1. Make sure the item you choose as your pointer has an easily visible tip (this is the area you'll be watching for results).

2. Make sure the item can be evenly weighted when suspended from string or yarn; uneven weighting can skew results. For example, if the area you need to search is toward the left, but you're over-weighted to the right, you could get sidetracked in that direction.

3. Make sure it's durable considering the conditions under which you're going to use it (herbs don't take well to rain, for example).

4. Have a length of string or yarn that's as long as the area from the tip of your hand to your elbow with a little extra with which to suspend the chosen item.

5. String your pointer securely.

The beauty of the pendulum is that you need not actually walk an area for it to work. You can use a map or a hand-drawn representation instead. Now you'll place your elbow outside the map or representation so the pendulum hangs above it. Think of your goal and watch for movement. The pendulum may keep going in one particular direction or will only circle around the right location (whereas if you're in the wrong region, it stays still).

Now, don't expect perfection right away! While some folks seem to have a natural aptitude for dowsing, most of us have to take the time to practice and learn. To begin, have a friend hide something in an area where it won't be disturbed. Go to that area with your chosen dowsing tool and visualize the item. Walk slowly across the land. I like to use concentric circles starting from the outside working inward (clockwise). You may find that just following your inner voice is better for you—so don't get hung up on a search pattern.

Try to remain open to all your senses, and be especially aware of little twitches in your dowsing tool. If the tool gets a "hit," check and see if you're right. If not, check again, moving a little to the right or left. If that's still not successful, there's no reason not to test-drive other dowsing tools, alternative times of the day, and so on. Bear in mind that a lot of things can influence your success or failure (such as unexpected distractions), so don't give up right away. In the immortal words of Buddha: practice, practice, practice!

Chapter 18

Drums, Rattles, and Tambourines

Only the drum is confident, it thinks the world has not changed.
—Robinson Jeffers

You may tear apart the baby's rattle and see what makes the noise inside, but there is a veil covering the unseen world which not the strongest man, nor even the united strength of all the strongest men that ever lived, could tear apart. Only faith, fancy, poetry, love, romance, can push aside that curtain and view and picture the supernal beauty and glory beyond.
—Francis P. Church

*Hey! Mr. Tambourine Man, play a song for me,
I'm not sleepy and there is no place I'm going to.
Hey! Mr. Tambourine Man, play a song for me,
In the jingle jangle morning I'll come followin' you.*
—Bob Dylan

Making noise—from the time we're infants until the time we move on to another existence, human life is filled with sound. For our most ancient ancestors those sounds could signal many things from a good hunt to danger ahead. Over time we learned that making certain sounds offered protection, not to mention a convenient means by which to communicate with each other over long distances. Among these methods we find whistling, clicking, and drumming.

As the human culture developed, the arts began to surface. These arts depended on the skills and implements available, so it's not surprising that percussion became part of music in every civilization. While the form of the item varied, its function to hold rhythm remained sure. What that rhythm implied depended greatly on the setting, era, and purpose for the music (or playing of the instrument). For the purpose of this chapter we'll be focusing on easily obtainable percussion tools: the drum, rattle, and tambourine. Know, however, that you have a wide variety of other potential items available to you should you wish to explore the potentials of percussion in magick beyond the pages of this book.

Drums

The fastest growing sub-community among Neo-Pagans is that of the drummers. The beating of a drum speaks to our tribal soul. It calls us back to the fire, back to community, and back to our hearts and hearths. The drum has been regarded as an important magickal and spiritual instrument for thousands of years. Symbolically Buddhists see the drum as vibrating with higher law, and Africans regard it as a representation of heart and personal magick. The Chinese write of drums as singing the songs of heaven, Hindus believe it resonates with the first sounds of creation, and in Japan it calls for us to pray.

These beliefs are accompanied by a wide variety of customs as to how a drum gets treated. Some tribal cultures, for example, would never think to lay a drum on the ground because it is respected similarly to elders. Other peoples never think to play another's drum without permission for fear of offending the indwelling spirit. In other traditions still, drums are used as tools for communing with spirits, healing the sick, augmenting weather and agricultural rituals, driving away evil spirits, and traveling the astral realm, just to name a few uses.

Religiously speaking, we see even more veneration for drums. Among the Greeks, for example, only a priest or priestess could sound iambic pentameter. This particular rhythm was regarded as very powerful in the way it affected people, so only those trusted souls could utilize it. Drums were also an important part of worship to Greek Deities, including Dionysus.

Another religious group, Shamans, employed drums to transport them safely through the Spirit realm. The beating of the drum acts as a helpmate to the Shaman in these rites, the sound bridging the gap between the here-and-now and mystical realms. That very same sound also helps the Shaman navigate the astral landscape, and becomes a landmark for finding their way back. Some Shamans also used drums in ecstatic rites, hunting rituals, soul retrieval, worship, rites of passage, and for vision quests (note here that when I speak of Shamanism, I'm talking of a global comparative).

One rather lovely religious custom comes to us from West Africa. Among several tribes it's thought that each Spirit bears a rhythm. The only way to call a specific Being, therefore, is to know that rhythm. As one plays, that Spirit uses the sound as a vehicle for manifestations. Once the Spirit arrives, the practitioner might then dance with his or her drum in celebration.

Sounding Out History

In the region of Czechoslovakia archaeological digs have uncovered clay drums dating to about 6000 B.C.E. Other explorations in Bulgaria and Mesopotamia have unearthed drums made in 4500 B.C.E. and 3000 B.C.E. respectively. This last date is also approximately when art begins illustrating the use of drums in Egypt, Assyria, China, India, and Persia. No matter the area, however, drums had both a social and a spiritual function.

Early drums were obviously not as refined as those we now enjoy. The tops were frequently made from hides, including those of lizards, fish, and snakes. In warring societies one might also find a human skin drumhead (which was a rather potent way to show power over one's enemy).

The huge diversity of drums around the world, and the way in which they developed is too expansive for a book of this nature. If you'd like to explore further (especially if you're interested in following the drummer's path) try reading *Sacred Beat: From the Heart of the Drum Circle* (Wesier, Red Wheel, 2003). This book shares the rich tradition of drums as a tool for personal and communal spiritual transformation.

Buying a Drum

In traveling, I have noted that there are more drum-making workshops available at festivals and gatherings. For those who cannot attend such a workshop, and who want a refined drum with which to work, buying a drum is the next best option. I do not, however, recommend you get your drum over the Internet. You need to feel a drum, hear it, sit with it, and get to know its unique spirit before knowing if it's the one for you. If you don't like the way your drum feels or sounds, you won't play it—it's really that simple.

Also consider your life's circumstances in your purchase. The African djembe is a wonderful drum, for example, but it has a very loud voice. This is not the best drum for apartment living unless you're willing to sheath it (put a thin leather cover over the top) and a piece of thick foam underneath the bottom. While this approach neatly tones your drum down to a level that might be acceptable to neighbors, it also shifts the energy of your drum, and the way it sounds. Larger djembes are not easy to travel with, and are fairly hefty. So if you want a drum that will go with you to festivals, fit in the overhead on airlines, and be easily carried around a large site, this might not be the drum for you. These kinds of considerations hold true no matter what drum you're considering.

Other things of which to be aware is how heat and cold will affect the head of your drum, whether or not the head needs regular treatment (or if it is waterproof), how difficult it is to tune the drum, and if you can easily get a protective carrying case for it. Because many drum circles occur at festivals, you want to safeguard your investment against bangs and weather issues.

Once you've narrowed your choices down, sit with each drum for a while. Hold it and breathe deeply. Listen to the beating of your heart, then tap on the drum. How does that vibration feel? Does it mesh with your own? Drumming is a partnership and a relationship between your spirit and that of the drum. And, just like a lover, you'll know when it's right.

Making a Drum

There are some easy ways to make drums that have a reasonable sound to them. One is simply taking a large water cooler jug and turning it upside down. If you want, experiment with leaving various amounts of water inside (capped solidly) and see how that changes the resulting tone until you find a sound you like, or a sound that mingles well with the other drummers with whom you're playing.

A second type of drum can be made by taking a large PCV piece (16 inches x 16 inches in diameter). Cover this with hide, mylar, or other synthetics. This cover will need to be glued or banded in place. I recommend the latter because that will allow you to better adjust the tone of the drum. Craft shops often sell needlework hoops in various sizes that have spring action. This would allow you to place it on the drum's head, slide the hoop over, and check the tone. From this point, if you're using a natural hide, you can tighten it further by using sinew and stitching one side of the hide to the other as you might lace up a dress. A leather punch and grommets will make this a longer-lasting effort. Note, however, that the sound you get isn't as nice as a more professionally made item.

Rattle

The first percussion instruments were human hands and feet. The second ones were rattles. More than likely, when humans started growing plants, someone picked up a dried gourd and shook it, hearing the sound. Because these rudimentary instruments came from the earth, there was no real lack in supply.

As early as approximately 2500 B.C.E., a sistrum (rattle-like instrument) had worked its way into worship and dances to honor Hathor. This same instrument appeared in the Bible as part of sacred processions. Ancient Greeks and Romans made rattles out of clay pots with tiny stones and dried beans inside. Meanwhile, Mediterranean cultures filled their rattles with bits of coral and fashioned handles out of coral, both of which were favored gifts for new parents. Even with all this history, it wasn't until the 1700s that rattles began to show up in advertising alongside the ever-popular whistle.

Shake, Rattle, and Roll

If you'd like to make a rattle, it's not that difficult. You could follow our ancestors' tradition and use a dried gourd, or you could go more modern and put some dry beans in a plastic food storage container. Note that if you're using the second method, you can adjust the sound by increasing or decreasing the amount of beans, or by changing the medium to something such as seeds or rice. Another way to vary the sound of the rattle is by laying threads with attached bells across the opening of the container (long enough so the bells extend beyond the bottom edge of the container). Put the top on, and now you have a blend of bells and a more traditional percussion sound.

Tambourine

Similar to drums and rattles, tambourines have a long history in various civilizations, including China, Egypt, India, and Rome. In the Bible, Miriam played a tambourine while the Israelites left Egypt (Exodus 15:20). In Islamic regions it's traditionally a woman's instrument. Overall, the symbolism in these cultures included happiness, success, and protection (as was the case with many noise-making implements).

149

This instrument was popularized in the 18th century when it even appeared in opera! By the 19th century, it found its way into many churches as a tool for praise and worship. And the Victorians even used the tambourine as a tool for contacting spirits. This system of divination called tympana was very simple. A tambourine was left on the table or hung in the room. If the instrument sounded when questions were posed, it indicated the spirit's response (positive or negative) by the number of taps.

Magickally speaking, I think the tambourine makes a wonderful implement for calling the East (because of the Air Element) and for celebrating at the Community Fire Circle.

For more information on percussion instruments I highly recommend these two Websites:

- *www.rhythmweb.com/homemade:* This is an excellent education Website for many types of percussion instruments.

- *www.thedrumworks.com:* This Website has excellent quality instruments at similarly good prices.

Chapter 19

Elemental Items

Modern man is battered by the elemental forces of his own psyche.
—Carl Jung

In talking about Wicca and a great number of Neo-Pagan traditions, something about the Elements nearly always enters the conversation. Our correspondences for the Four Directions, for every plant and stone in the world, and even for personalities, begin with the Elements of Earth, Air, Fire, Water, and Spirit. For the purpose of this chapter it's easiest to discuss each separately and how you might represent these energies in your life and sacred spaces.

Air

Air is the most elusive of the Elements. We know we breathe, but the only time we can "see" that breath is when it is cold outside. We know the wind blows, as evidenced only by the trees, and grass. moved by the breeze's hand. Consequently, the Ancients looked at the Air Element as being somewhat changeable, unknowable, and curious.

Metaphysically we have to look at Air on two levels—within and without. Within, it's the vital breath, theoretical thoughts, intangible insights, and psychic gifts that are just as persnickety. The wind of the Divine also fuels the fire of our souls as an ongoing nudge to move, to do, to be.

Externally, Air connects with our speech and hearing—our ability to communicate to, and understand communication from, our environment effectively. The spoken or sung word, mantras, the cry of animals, the bird in flight—these are all Air, and each is worthy of a study unto itself. Because most Wiccans consider East/Air the starting point of creating sacred space, pondering the significance of creation by word and sound is a very worthy endeavor.

Because of its nature, Air isn't quite as "solid" as the other Elements. However, a creative Kitchen Witch can find ways to use this tool effectively, including:

- ♋ Aromatherapy: Let the winds carry your intentions magickally and subconsciously.

- ♋ Breathing: An integral part of meditation and any centering work, learning to work with your body's breathing patterns is very helpful to spiritual endeavors.

- ♋ Cast it to the winds: Be it herbs that you toss with a wish, or a symbolic item intended to carry sickness away from you, let Air be an Element of movement in your life.

- ♋ Open a new window: Fresh air improves awareness, health, and overall ambiance.

⁋ Air it out: When you need a transformation, open the window, and let the winds of change move into your life.

A New Wind

We can't "make" wind per se, but thanks to the wonders of modern technology a fan can! This tool lets you also direct the air from a specific location or toward another region, depending on your goal. For example, if you want to inspire passion in a spell, you might "fan the flames" from the South a bit!

Fire

Before we gathered in circles around a communal flame, there was the Sun shining overhead. Daytime was far safer for our ancestors. The Sun's warmth offered comfort, and light for hunting, gathering, and dispelling night's shadows to reveal Earth's beauty.

When a miracle from the sky brought fire down, it's no wonder it became a sacred item. I can't help but think it was a primitive Kitchen Witch who first accidentally dropped food therein! In any case, once found and kept as a treasure for the hearth, the symbolic nature of fire was one of power, safety, and kinship. In rituals and spellcraft it appeared as a partner in seasonal rites, and efforts for abundance, inspiring fertility, divination, protection, love, and luck (just to name a few).

Fire resides in the South of the magickal circle and it is governed by the solar disk (no great surprise there). Where Water and the Moon are most often feminine in nature, Fire is typically masculine—the yang to the yin. Thankfully, in its forms Fire was not as shy as Air in revealing itself:

જ Ashes: I know many communities who collect ashes and a live coal from each gathering and keep them safe until the next event. This truly honors the heart as the heart—no matter where it resides. By the way, you can use ashes as a Fire Element representation in portable altars.

જ Candles: We've talked about these extensively earlier the book.

જ Fires (fireplace, bonfire): An incredible earthly symbol of the Fire above, neatly illustrating the "as above so below" axiom. A wonderful place to scry, burn away those things you don't need, reenergize, and inspire yourself.

જ Lightbulbs: The modern convenience that can also symbolically represent the Sun. In my house I get broad spectrum bulbs and bless them for happiness during months when I often struggle with seasonal depression. Dab a little meaningful oil on yours, then light up your wishes!

જ Let the sun shine: Put up sheer curtains in your home or sacred spaces using colors that accentuate your goals and then let the Sun do part of the work for you by shining that colored light throughout!

Light My Fire

Thanks to matches, stoves, and lighters we don't have quite the same task as our ancestors when it comes to fire building. However, I do encourage readers to try building a fire a few times. For one thing, it builds respect for the Element, and as someone who never considered herself very outdoorsy, it was a boost to my self-confidence to discover the wonders of this art.

My suggestion for any fire is to begin with what would be considered full-sized pieces for your area—you obviously need more for an outdoor fire than inside for a fireplace. Put those down along with any candle ends and pieces you have. On top of this, pile kindling and crumpled paper. After you light the paper the fire should build neatly from the top down with very little smoke. While this is but one approach, it's a tried and true method to which many people ascribe.

Water

Eons ago when the Wheel of Life began to turn, life emerged from the ancient oceans. Our myths handed down from various cultures support this transition, sharing how the seas even birthed some of the gods and goddesses. This makes Water a spiritual and tribal "home" for humankind. It's no wonder that we feel drawn to water much as our ancestors did.

As human communities developed many of life's important moments, water was sprinkled around sacred spaces to bless and cleanse. People washed their hands and bodies in water before entering the temple. Townspeople gathered at wells and left offerings to appease spirits (the origins of the wishing well). Healers used water as part of their rites, lovers oathed near running water, and women gathered May Day dew to ensure beauty.

Metaphysically most practitioners consign Water to the Western portion of creation (unless they happen to live closely to water that's in a different direction), under the ruling of the Moon. The most common tool associated with this Element is the cup or bowl already discussed in Chapter 9. However, I'd like to look at water a slightly different way. What about this Element itself? Because nearly everyone has indoor plumbing these days, water is a very readily available and functional tool.

Better still, it has a variety of forms, giving it even more symbolic value. Consider:

- ෂ Dew: Since the Middle Ages this was collected for beauty and wealth at specific times of the year (possible because it was associated with Fairy activity).

- ෂ Fog: Oh, what fun for Samhain rituals (mind you we have to cheat a bit and use dry ice!).

- ෂ Ice: What do you want to slow or halt? Put it in ice! Or, for safety, write your name on a piece of paper and place it in the tray with water. Just be careful not to serve that cube to a guest accidentally!

- ෂ Rain: Our forbearers used it in healing and blessing rites regularly (it also can represent nourishment and cleansing).

- ෂ Snow: Hey, no two flakes are alike, so use this in creativity spells.

- ෂ Sweat: A very personal thing that can be utilized to "mark" your magickal tools.

- ෂ Steam: Because the smoke from fires and incense has been used for years to convey prayers, why not steam from the Kitchen Witch's cooking pot?

With all this in mind, Water often participates in rituals and spells to support the goals of fertility, friendship, purification, forgiveness, insight, emotions, patience, and the psychic nature.

Boiling Water?

It's obvious that you don't need to "make" this particular tool as you can get it from any sink or collect it on a rainy day. You can also go to the ocean, or set out a cloth on a humid night to gather dew. But don't stop there. You can scent water (such as making special finger bowls with aromas that match your magickal meal), color the water for vases on your altar, and drop crystals in water to create stone elixirs. For inspiring the child within, jump in puddles while reciting "rain, rain, go away, this little Witch wants to play" or when its hot out, dance with the asperging water from a neighborhood sprinkler. Contrary to old myths, real Kitchen Witches don't melt!

Earth

We are of one world—a living, breathing, and vivid Being. Early humans often made their home in caves. From this place of relative safety, they ventured to hunt, to gather, to discover. A little at a time, we encountered the wonders of our world, and each other.

As an Element, Earth touches all others. It cannot help but do so. Air is Gaia's breath, Water provides nourishment to all the Earth's creatures, and the Sun warms our soil. When you hold a handful of rich loam, you hold all the potential of creation. That, my friends, is real magick!

Metaphysically speaking, we consign Earth to the Northern Quarter of creation with the attributes of grounding, foundations, growth, frugality, and abundance. Our ancestors also often oathed by Earth, and used soil in healing, love, prosperity, luck, and divinatory rites. Better still, for us, Earth also bears more than one form!

- Clay: The stuff from which humankind was made if you ascribe to Genesis. This appears most often in healing and beauty magick

- Dust: Some people divined by dust (makes me wonder what my coffee table is trying to tell me). Others used dust from sacred sites and crossroads for health and longevity charms.

- ᎓ Stones: Plain stones are a perfect representation of solid foundations. If you find a stone with a hole in it, that's lucky and considered a blessing.
- ᎓ Salt: Cleansing and protection, and thanks to the phrase "worth his salt," also a good Earth component for fostering appreciation and financial security.
- ᎓ Sand: An excellent medium within which to burn herbs and incense. If you're under the weather and near the beach, bury yourself in warm sand for a while. Visualize your malady being left in the sand.
- ᎓ Soil: Another item used in healing rituals and also a great medium for when you want something to "grow" in your life.

Finally, one of my personal favorite ways to represent Earth in a vital, living form is through potted plants. I'll sow flowers (for example) in Elemental colors for the Four Quarters as a way to celebrate Earth Day. It's also now known that having live plants in your home helps allay various psychological problems such as seasonal depression (hey, Kitchen Witches support multitasking!).

Chapter 20

Food

A dining room table with children's eager, hungry faces around it ceases to be a mere dining room table and becomes an altar.

—Simeon Strunsky

Be it a simple kitchen table around which a family gathers for meal time prayer or a fanciful altar where hundreds come to worship, food has participated in religious rituals and spiritual practices for thousands of years. Starting with hearth and home, the kitchen assumed a place of honor in many cultural settings to the point where the hearth fire was the first area of a home built. Allowing that fire to go out was considered a very ill omen.

I am willing to bet that if you think about your families, you'll be able to come up with some meal-oriented recipes or mini-rituals that you enacted for special holidays and observances. That's the perfect place to begin pondering food's function in your metaphysical practices as a tool. We can also look to how other people have used it in a more formal religious manner at home.

Pantry and Food Altars

Perhaps one of the best examples of a kitchen altar comes to us from China, where many people keep a special spot set apart for the Kitchen God. This Deity oversees all matters of ethics in the home all year long, then reports this information to the Jade Emperor on Chinese New Years. It's not surprising, therefore, to find this altar strewn with all kinds of sweet offerings so that the God's report will be sweet as well.

Other examples of kitchen altars that have a food focus include:

- Sicilian altars or statuary for St. Joseph who insures the family will never want for food.
- India, where the Vedic tradition considers the kitchen an extension of the altar. It's not uncommon to find people carefully preparing offerings for Lakshmi, Narayana, Sita, Rama, Radha, and Krishna here (see also Food for the Gods later in this chapter).
- Japan and Korea, where people often keep ancestral altars in the kitchen so that the spirits of the departed can be close to the family.

This gives an aspiring Kitchen Witch some good ideas with which to begin. If you plan to create a small altar space in your kitchen on which to bless and energize various meals or food components, you'll likely want it as close to the stove (the hearth/heart) as possible. If you can't do that, try the microwave (it's a modern equivalent) or a sunny window (symbolizing emotional warmth).

Because we already discussed setting up altars in another chapter, I won't belabor the point, but when talking about food as a tool, the concept of a kitchen altar makes sense, even if you only consider it your countertop! Another suitable use for a kitchen altar is as a place to leave small food offerings for various Deities, or bless foods intended to honor gods and goddesses in ritual or on the dining room table. Let's take a look at this idea more closely.

Food for the Gods

It was pretty common for the Ancients to petition a suitable Deity for help in the hunt or with crop growth. So when the harvest came it's not surprising to discover those very same people offering part of the Earth's bounty back to the Creators by way of thanks. In fact, the Wiccan holiday known as Lammas is based on the tradition where the first sheaf of wheat or first loaf of bread is set aside for good luck and as a sign of gratitude for Divine blessings.

Lammas Bread Recipe

Lammas means "loaf mass," and while you could use any bread recipe you wish, one good option is corn bread because this is a grain crop traditionally harvested around this time of year where the holiday falls. However, if you happen to have a busy work schedule, no one ever said preparing your food tools would have to take a ton of time, thanks to modern boxed goods! In this case, take a box of Jiff Corn Muffin mix and prepare it according to directions, adding a pinch of sugar for life's sweetness, and a bit of orange rind so the bread has a lovely golden color. Place in the suitable size baking dish (well greased and lightly floured). Gently draw a symbol that, to you, represents abundance. Pour the batter in and bake per the instructions on the box, remembering to give the first slice to the Divine or to a guest in your home, which is also a good way to share the magick.

In addition to using food to thank and honor the gods, people felt that various gods and goddesses held specific food items as sacred (that is, the myths and customs of the Deity were somehow intertwined with that item). This makes specific food groups or items the perfect implement to add to our sacred spaces when calling upon various Divine visages. The food in this case acts like a letter of welcome, and can even represent the God or Goddess being invoked in lieu of a statue or candle. Here's a brief list of foods, spices, and the beings connected to them for your reference:

Food	*God or Goddess*
Almond	Artemis (Greece)
	Ptah (Egypt)
Apple	Hera and Zeus (Greece)
Banana	Kanaloa (Hawaii)
Barley	Indra (India)
	Demeter (Greece)
Basil	Vishnu (India)
Bay	Eros and Apollo (Greece)
	Faunus (Rome)
Beans	Apollo (Rome)
Beef	Hathor (Egypt)
Beet	Aphrodite (Grece)
Bread	Isis (Egypt)
Broccoli	Jupiter (Rome)
Cinnamon	Dionysus (Greece)
Coconut	Hina (Hawaii)
	Ganymede (Greece)

Food	*God or Goddess*
Corn	Quetzalcoatl (Aztec)
	Cerridwen (Wales)
Crab	Apollo (Greece)
Dates	Ea (Babylon)
	Artemis (Greece)
Egg	Shiva (India)
	Venus (Rome)
Fig	Ra and Isis (Egypt)
	Juno (Greece)
Fish	Poseidon (Rome)
	Isis and Ra (Egypt)
Game meat	Artemis (Greece)
Garlic	Hecate (Greece)
Grapes	Bacchus (Rome)
Honey	Ra (Egypt)
	Persephone (Phoenicia)
Lobster	Ares (Greece)
Mango	Buddha (China)
Marjoram	Aphrodite (Greece)
Milk	Hathor (Egypt)
Mint	Pluto (Rome)
Nettle	Thor (Germany)
Olive	Minerva (Rome)
Pear	Athena (Greece)
Pomegranate	Zeus and Ceres (Greece)
Rice	Inari (Japan)
Saffron	Brahma (Hindu)
Salt	Tiamat (Sumer)
Sesame	Ganesha (India)

Food	*God or Goddess*
Strawberry	Freya (Germany)
Sunflower	Helios (Greece)
Water	Ea (Chaldea)
Watermelon	Set (Egypt)
Wheat	Ishtar (Meso-Babylon)
Wine	Ishtar (Meso-Babylon)
	Osirus and Isis (Egypt)
	Dionysus (Greece)

Obviously, this list is dramatically abbreviated, but you get the idea.

As a side note for Divine food, many people felt that eating an item sacred to a specific Being could also act as a means of communing with that Being. An excellent example of this comes to us from Greece where the followers of Bacchus felt that he was present any time wine was poured. And upon drinking the wine, one could become possessed. This is actually part of the reason we call alcohol "spirits" to this day (see also Chapter 29).

Edible Alchemy

Beyond various edibles significant to the Divine, we also have a plethora of metaphysical correspondences to consider so that we can use this tool in our magickal practices. We can choose a food or a mixture of foods for the inherent mystical energies so when we eat the food, we "internalize" that significance. Or we can add the food to our spells, charms, and rituals similarly.

As with any other tool, you want to consider its intended function in your magick. Dry goods (such as beans, coffee, and herbs, for example, are far better for charms and amulets than anything that's raw, ripe, or cooked because it is more easily transported without a mess. On the other hand, fresh food might be more apt to the altar or Quarter points, as would live, food-bearing plants. In this case, the freshness represents a similarly fresh, vibrant source of energy. Somehow I can't quite see the Ancients giving the gods an offering of rotten meat or fruit!

This book's space doesn't allow for an extensive listing of metaphysical food correspondences. Instead, I suggest you consider first what that item represents to you. For example, most people think of chicken soup and apples as inspiring health and renewal. The soup does more good as a "potion," whereas dried apple or apple seeds could easily be part of a portable health talisman.

If you're not certain as to a food's magickal value, you can refer to books such as my *Kitchen Witch's Cookbook* (Llewelyn Publications, 2002), *Kitchen Witch's Companion* (Citadel Press, 2005), or you could consider the item's color or aromatic correspondence instead. Here are two lists to which you can quickly refer for these two options.

Color Values

- Red Food: eat for energy, passion, and fire-oriented goals
- Green Food: consume for hope, happiness, steady growth, and abundance
- Orange Food: enjoy for developing friendships, new skills, and alertness
- White Food: internalize for lunar energy, purity, and insightfulness
- Yellow Food: nibble to strengthen faith, communication skills, and creativity

Aromatic Values

Note: These values are based on my personal interpretation of metaphysical energies combined with aromatherapy values. Aromatherapy typically focuses more heavily on aromatic herbs than foods, thus the adaptation.

- Anise: psychic energy, and divination
- Garden snap peas: friendship
- Citrus: energy, awareness, conscious energy, and cleansing
- Basil: peace and love
- Bread (especially freshly baked): comfort, and providence
- Berries: abundance, prosperity, and fertility
- Rosemary: healing and memory
- Cinnamon: good fortune
- Tomato sauce: love and kinship
- Nutmeg: focus and insight
- Vanilla: passion
- Warm milk: healing and nurturing

Again, I would remind readers that while these values have very strong meanings for me, each item on this list could carry a different symbolism to you based on your personal experiences and insights. Please, always trust those first gut instincts.

Divination

Last, but certainly not least, another way to utilize food as a tool-teacher is in divination efforts. Two familiar forms of food divination are scrying coffee creamer or tea leaves. In the first instance the questioner usually stirs the creamer once clockwise while thinking of his or her question and then observes the surface for images to appear. In the second instance the questioner thinks about the question while drinking tea made from loose leaves. The remaining pattern in the bottom of the cup is then observed. Both methods are very similar to trying to find the images in an inkblot.

Here are just a few more food items people used for divination:

1. Bread: If you drop your toast butter-side down, you'll soon have guests. Baking two loaves of bread together and having them join portends good things for relationships and perhaps a marriage. Cutting bread unevenly speaks of difficult discussions, and crumbling bread predicts arguments.

2. Beans: Greeks used black and white beans for simple yes or no type questions. To try this yourself, put an even number of black and white beans in a bag or bowl. Think of a question, close your eyes, and draw out one bean. If you'd like to reconfirm that answer, draw two more beans. A mix of more black than white is negative, all black is an absolute no (or not now). You can also use more than two colors to allow for a greater variety of answers to your question, such as using yellow beans to symbolize something that needs to be discussed, green beans for financial matters, and red beans for love or passion.

3. Cheese: Another method originally from both Greece and Rome, the next time you slice Swiss cheese, count the number of holes you see. If the number is even, the weeks ahead will be positive.

4. Egg: Europeans in the 1600s poked a hole in one end of an egg and then held it over water. The patterns that emerged while thinking of one's question was interpreted very similarly to tea leaves.

5. Flour: Yet another Grecian method, the priestess of Apollo sprinkled flour on water and interpreted the patterns created. You could do this on a damp countertop surface.

6. Oil: Divination by oil originated in the Middle East where it's likely that olive oil would have been used. As with the Grecian flour method, the oil gets added to a bowl of water and its movement interpreted. The interpretations here, however, more strongly resemble those in candle scrying (for example, a glob of oil dividing is a negative omen often implying some type of divide or separation).

If you'd like to explore divination with food in a little more detail, try reading *Kitchen Witch's Guide to Divination* (New Page, 2004). Or if you're a Kitchen Witch looking for recipes try *Kitchen Witch's Companion* (Citadel Press, 2005).

See also the chapters on altars and offerings (Chapters 2 and 26).

Chapter 21

Herbs and Plants

He who plants a tree, plants a hope.

—Lucy Larcom

You'd be hard pressed to find a Kitchen Witch without a cupboard filled with a variety of dried herbs and plants. Above and beyond their obvious function in cooking, plants are keynote components in spells, rituals, meditative incense, divinatory efforts, and so on. Akin to candles, these are among the most useful and easily obtained items in the Witch's tool kit.

Herbal History

In recent years we've experienced an amazing rebirth in herbal arts. It seems that perhaps our ancestors weren't silly in using Nature's pharmacy to cure, let alone for magick. Since the beginning of time, humans turned to Nature for food, but as we did this we also found that some plants seemed to have odd effects on our bodies. Some seemed to relieve pain, others increased perspiration, and so on. As we made the connection between the plant and its physical affects, the art of herbalism was born.

The first written records of herbs in medicine comes to us from Mesopotamia (Iraq). Thousands of years ago, Sumerian physicians were prescribing caraway and thyme for various ailments. They weren't alone. Chinese medicine has herbal strictures going back 5,000 years, and the knowledge of more than 500 medicinal plants was documented in India as early as 800 B.C.E. The Greeks gave us Hippocrates (the father of medicine circa 400 B.C.E.) who taught, "Let your foods be your medicines, and your medicines your food." I would be so bold as to take that statement one step further saying, "Let your foods be your magick!"

European monks continued the herbal traditions, and when Europeans arrived in America they added Native American knowledge to the repository. Lewis and Clark in particular set a goal of learning from the Native Americans about beneficial herbs. Globally speaking, however, we should remind ourselves that every part of the world has seen the development of some type of herbal art based on along with indigenous plants, those items that came through trade and exploratory routes.

Of course, many of these arts had a healthy portion of superstition mingled therein. Modern methods have tried to carefully discern what was "belief" and what was truly effective. From a spiritual perspective, the rituals and religious rites connected with the superstitions are important in terms of honoring metaphysical energies. This makes a delicate balancing act for our forward-thinking Kitchen Witch that must take care with potential health issues when whipping up any internalized item for magickal ends. Thankfully, there are numerous books that provide us with both the benefits and potential problems with various herbs. My best suggestion is to have one medical herbalism book, one metaphysical herbal book, and one historical book. This will provide you with an excellent foundation for all your efforts.

Compost or Component?

I keep ends and pieces of nearly everything from my garden and my cooking efforts if it's feasible. To my mind, waste is very un-Witchy. So if you peek in my freezer you're likely to find rose petals gathered at various astrological times alongside extra bay leaves! Both are edible, and both have a wide variety of applications in my magick.

Plants and herbs have played a vital role in spellcraft and rituals for a very long time. It's fairly safe to say that there's likely not a green-growing thing in this world that someone, somewhere, hasn't tried to use for metaphysical purposes. Exactly how an item got chosen for specific goals (at least initially) is the subject of some conjecture. However, more than likely, early humans looked to the shape of the plant, its color, and what they knew of it mundanely for their decisions. Later, as humans began to pass along magickal herbalism verbally or in written form, we saw this decision-making process as a tradition. For example, the heart-shaped leaf would be used in spells for love or to heal a broken heart. It makes sense based on the laws of like attracting like.

These days we don't have to use quite so much guesswork, thanks to the hundreds of people before us who have experimented with a variety of plants and herbs in their magick. Nonetheless, I strongly urge Kitchen Witches to trust their instincts. Even if a rose has been used for thousands of years to inspire love, and even if it's recommended in a spell you're planning to utilize, remember that personal meaningfulness is still important. If a plant or herb has a different meaning for you, that meaning has to be honored somehow in your working. Otherwise you'll have no emotional and mental connection to the symbolic value of that item, and the magick won't work right, if at all.

The answer to this quandary is component substitution, a time-honored method among Witches. There are some cautions, however:

- If this spell or potion is meant for consumption, make sure that the plant or herb you use is (a) consumable, (b) doesn't cause allergic reactions, and (c) maintains continuity with the goal of your working.

- If you're making a libation, offering, charm, etc. that is not for consumption, please label accordingly so there are no potential accidents.

- Remember that the growing conditions for plants and herbs can change their energies. For example, the rose that's harvested during a hot summer at noon is going to have more "fire" energy than one harvested during a rainy season by moonlight. Listen to the voice of your plant's spirit for guidance!

Having said all that, plant parts and herbs are fantastic for nearly everything magickal. Here are just a few ideas:

- Break them into small pieces for burning or making into charms.

- Place Elemental plants and herbs around the sacred space as part of invocation.

- Scatter herbs to the winds with your wishes, or on water to carry your goals to the Four Corners of creation.

- Toss meaningful aromatic plants into the dryer with your clothing to charge your aura as you put those items on for the day.

- Add plant tinctures to household wash water to charge everything you clean with magick.
- Create a special mixture of plant parts for portable amulets and talismans.
- Select herbs for magickal potions and teas (all the spices you have in your pantry have magickal correspondences).

Botanomancy

Like so many other of the Kitchen Witch's tools, plants and herbs are magickal multitaskers! Some have been associated with divinatory practices, too. Here are just a few examples:

- Go into the yard and pick a clover. If it has two leaves, you'll soon meet someone that you'll love, or with whom you'll create a partnership.
- Place a birthday candle on a holly leaf in water. If the leaf floats, this portends prosperity on the horizon.
- If you find a sprig of sage, it's an omen of good luck.
- Choose a flower that represents your yes or no question. Put this in the bottom of a bowl. Slowly pour water into the bowl while thinking of your question. If the flower floats, your answer is yes.
- Plant geraniums near your front door. Watch to see which directions the blossoms turn when in full bloom. This is the direction from which you'll receive guests.
- Use a holly leaf with eight candles to receive prophetic dreams. Just tuck them under your pillow

on Samhain. An alternative to this is using mistletoe on Yule.

☙ If you find myrtle growing near your door, it predicts happiness and peace in the home.

☙ Burn five bay leaves bundled together. Think of a yes or no question. If they burn noisily, the answer is yes. This may also be done using two basil leaves. If they burn slowly, there's supportive energy. If they snap and pop, beware of arguments.

☙ Tie a sprig of a symbolic herb to a string and use it as a pendulum to find the answer to a question. (see Chapter 17).

Whenever possible I do suggest that Kitchen Witches grow their own herbs. It doesn't take a lot of space, and it allows you to feed each item with the energies desired. I often put a hanging crystal over my potted herbs to increase the effects (such as having an amethyst dangling over lavender plants or a pink quartz over basil). Better still, if you're growing your own, you can harvest the plants at astrologically auspicious times that will support your goals. For those without space for this, you can shop for your herbs during auspicious times instead (to my mind, shopping is a modern version of "gathering").

Chapter 22

Incense and Censers

I breathe in the cool incense smoke from the metal brazier,
While thinking about a poem for my dear friend Lu Wa.
My sandalwood-hearted companion spits out plum blossoms of
smoke, looking like the cloudy fog of the other world.
Perhaps it's the soul of my friend the old mountain man
In the smoke's dense patterns?

—Kan Po, in memoriam

The smell of sage and sweetgrass is wellknown to Wiccans everywhere. They're among the most popular smudging herbs for sacred spaces (at least at the Circles I've attended). Additionally, we use incense to aid in meditation, shift the vibrations in our homes, and inspire the energies of our auras both personally and in group work. Where does our use of incense originate? Very likely in humankind's ancient past and the religious practices of many people.

Smoke in the Wind: Incense and History

The first experience humans had with incense likely came alongside our exposure to fire. As various woods burned with plant matter, we'd notice that some smelled good and others not so good. Because the care of fire was often given to a special person in the ancient tribes such as a Shaman, it is not surprising that this aromatic tradition quickly became tangled with medicine and magick. In many settings incense-making was considered a sacred art.

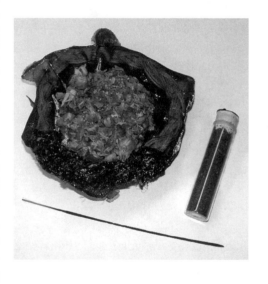

Traditionally, incense has been made from dried wood or bark, plant seeds, flowers, spices, and resins, such as myrrh. These aromatics and others played important roles in Egyptian, Vedic, Hindu, Shinto, and Buddhist rituals. We find notation of incense being used in India around 5000 B.C.E.! The ancient Greek writings make note of it around the eigth century B.C.E.

Buddhism came to Japan in 538 C.E., and with it came incense. From that point forward incense, especially aloeswood, sandalwood, and clove blends, became an integral part of the history of Japan, being used in religion and medicine. When those aromatics were not available, suitable substitutions were patchouli, cassia, and cinnamon. Incense cones were introduced to the United States by Japan at the 1800 World's Fair. To their credit, some of the most complex and expensive incense continues to come from Japan via import, and the incense ceremony called Kodo continues to be practiced (it takes more than 30 years to learn this art).

During the Middle Ages, mainstream churches began using incense widely. This had a pragmatic function too. It covered the smell of people who, thanks to superstition, didn't bathe regularly. Additionally, many healers felt that burning herbs decreased disease. We know today that many of the herbs used did indeed have an anti-bacterial or cleansing effect.

Around the 18th century, the art of perfumery had an influence on incense by bringing synthetic ingredients and mechanized methods into the equation. It's interesting to note that the word *perfume* means "through smoke," which shows how intimately these two are related.

Making Incense

Magickally speaking, your blend will be created for its associated energy. However, it's nice if it smells good, too! Many incense ingredients have little or no smell until they're hot or burning. That means you need to begin judiciously with your experiments.

The first step in making incense is determining if you want combustible incense or incense that requires an external fire source. Combustible incense requires the addition of specific material that will make it easier to burn. This type of incense can additionally be shaped into cones, patties, and sticks.

Noncombustible incense, by comparison, is often loose so that you can sprinkle the desired amount on charcoal or into a fire.

Noncombustible incense is far easier to make, but requires a fire-safe container and fire source. For this purpose I often use a sturdy wood bowl or large shell filled with sand on top of a trivet or other protective surface. This type of container is a good choice for combustible incense, too.

Now on to the next step: gathering your equipment. For both types of incense you'll want your burner, ingredients, a grinder or mortar and pestle, mixing bowls that you don't use for food, measuring tools, waxed paper, a spoon, and matches. In choosing your ingredients, I suggest starting with no more than three organic aromatics, at least one of which should be a resin or wood. All three choices should match your goal. After a few trial runs, you can make your recipes more complex, but this way you don't use a lot of ingredients only to discover you hate the results.

To make loose incense, the most important factor is that your ingredients are of approximately the same size. Use a grinder or mortar to powder each item separately, then blend them together. Be aware that commercial coffee grinders sometimes get too hot for this purpose (releasing essential oils/aromas) and usually aren't strong enough to tackle resins. Additionally, working the herbs by hand gives you extra time to focus on your intention and put that energy into the final product. What about wood? I use an old pencil sharpener to grind mine, or just buy powdered wood from the get-go. In any case, try blending the mix together in equal proportions, and then let it age for a few weeks so that the aromas integrate. Test this on a fire source to make sure you like the scent. You can add a few drops of aromatic oils to increase the fragrance, or add more wood powder to tone down the scent.

Transforming your loose mixture into pellets isn't too difficult. To your base you can add dried fruit, a little honey, wine, labdanum, and/or a pliable resin so that the mix becomes doughy. Don't add much more than half a cup of these additions per full cup of dried mix. As before, you want your additions to be of similar size as the powder. Mash everything together and knead. You'll notice as you work the mix it becomes crumbly. That's the texture you want. Leave this to dry overnight on a piece of wax paper inside a box top (this way bits don't get all over your counter top). Just please keep this out of reach of pets and children, as it needs about three weeks of turning and drying to finish.

Moving from the loose incense to cones, sticks, and pellets that are combustible, you'll need to add saltpeter or powdered charcoal. By far, saltpeter is less messy. Here's one recipe:

6 cups wood powder (sandalwood, cedar, pine)

2 cups benzoin, myrr, or other resin

1 cup orris root

10 drops essential oil

4 cups powdered (loose) incense

Mix all your ingredients together, making sure they're well combined and very evenly powdered. Weigh this. Whatever the weight, add saltpeter in the proportion of 10 percent and mix thoroughly again. Next add tragacanth glue a little at a time until the mix appears to resemble stiff cookie dough. You can now shape cones or patties easily. This needs to dry for about a week, and then store it in a dark, air-tight container for longevity.

Libanomancy

Libanomancy is any form of divination that requires the use of incense, either in the ritualistic portion of the effort or as the item for observation. In the case of the former, the chosen incense burns to heighten awareness. For the latter, the diviner observes the smoke from the burning incense looking for clues to the question at hand. Normally, smoke that moves up and to the right reflects a positive answer. Smoke moving down and left is negative, and if the incense won't light it's a very bad omen. Most of the interpretive values for pyromancy also applies to libanomancy. Just substitute the word "smoke" for "flame."

Chapter 23

Mirrors

Just as a mirror may be used to reflect images, so ancient events may be used to understand the present.

—Chinese proverb

Throughout the world, mirrors have a variety of symbolic value. In Western society, for example, the mirror represents ego and shallowness. Yet in an odd dichotomy, it may also represent truth because "the mirror never lies." Across the world in the Middle East, however, mirrors are sacred to the goddesses of beauty. Hindus see a mirror as an emblem of the human capacity to grow beyond mortal limitations and become spiritually aware. In Japan it's a symbol of the Sun, and in China mirrors characterize a happy life, especially in relationships.

For Kitchen Witches, mirrors offer a wide variety of symbolic value to a similarly wide variety of workings. For example, a mirror turned outward can send away unwanted energies. A mirror with a candle before it becomes a meditative tool and a means of contacting spirits. A small mirror might become a charm to improve one's self-esteem, while another could be blessed for truth-seeing. No matter what, as you read, keep your mind open. A mirror isn't just for scrying anymore!

History's Reflection

Humankind's first mirrors were things such as the surface of water that naturally reflected images. Later, when society developed metal, that polished surface became the first crude mirror, often fashioned from bronze. It wasn't until the first century C.E. that large mirrors appeared, often made with silver. By the seventh century, mirrors were being made out of glass.

The metallic backing for mirrors developed between the 12th and 13th centuries, followed by a mirror industry developing in Venice during the 14th to 15th centuries. It was during this era that the famed Catherine De Medici used a scrying mirror to look to the future. One century later, John Dee could be found scrying with mirrors in Queen Elizabeth's court!

From this point onward, mirrors became more widely refined and an item of artistic expression, often made with frames of rich woods and decorated with gems. However, when freestanding mirrors could be made less expensively come the 19th century, some of the fanciness went away with demand from everyday consumers who wanted a mirror as part of their homes.

Mirror Superstitions

- If a couple catches sight of each other in a mirror accidentally on their wedding day, they will have a happy marriage.
- If a mirror falls and breaks, it's an omen of death or dramatic changes.

- ꙮ Cover a mirror after a person has died so that their spirit cannot use it to return and haunt the home.
- ꙮ Babies should not look into a mirror for the first year of their lives.
- ꙮ Dreaming of a cloudy mirror speaks of confusion.
- ꙮ Cover a mirror in a thunderstorm to protect the house from lightning strikes.
- ꙮ Keep a mirror by your door to keep malicious spirits from entering the home.

Making a Magick Mirror

I think there's a tendency to think of a magick mirror as one that you only use for scrying. This is a pity, because mirrors have so many potential applications in magick. So while I'm going to tell you how to make a simple scrying mirror in this book, don't let that limit you. Also use mirrors:

- ꙮ In spellcraft (compact ones make great portable charms or part of witch bottles)
- ꙮ To direct energy in ritual (make one for every Quarter to honor the Elements and as a doorway for guardian energies)
- ꙮ As a meditative tool
- ꙮ In adjusting the energies of your sacred space by turning a mirror's surface where you want energy directed

For a scrying mirror, the first thing you'll need is to go to a dollar store and buy a picture frame with glass in it. If you're new to scrying, darker frames seem to make initial attempts more successful. Or, if you prefer, get a variety of frames so that the color or shape of each symbolizes the kinds of questions you plan to ask. Cabbalists actually made seven different mirrors, one for every day of the week, so this idea has some great magickal history behind it. For example, you could locate a wooden, square mirror and only use it for Earth-oriented or financial questions. Or you might find a yellow-framed mirror and set it aside for those times when you're scrying about communication matters. By the way, I've found really amazing frames for under $30 everywhere from flea markets to second-hand shops. Don't be afraid to look around and shop frugally! The cost of the mirror doesn't matter—what you do with it does!

You're also going to need a can of black, dark purple, forest green, or midnight blue enamel spray paint. Make sure this can be used on glass. I prefer high gloss, but if you're sensitive to light, you

may find a flat coat better. This type of paint is readily available at most department stores and hardware stores. If you're already at the store, grab some finely powdered glitter, too. Even if you end up not wanting it for the mirror, Kitchen Witches rarely have enough glitter!

Now remove the glass from the frame and clean it on both sides. Let it dry on a lint-free surface. This is a good juncture at which to metaphysically purify the exterior frame by smudging it or washing it with salt water. If you think about how many people handled this item before you, it is easy to see why this is a good precaution. You don't want random energy entering into the fabrication process.

Next, take a large piece of brown paper or cardboard and put it where you're going to be painting the glass. Carefully picking up the glass by the edges so as to keep it free of fingerprints, put this in the center of your working area. Spray the entire surface of the glass using even strokes. Avoid working where there's wind, or the paint will run, possibly causing lumps. Do not put more than one coat of paint on at a time on. Let this dry completely, then reapply. I usually like three or four coats because each application gives more depth perception (something that helps in scrying).

If you're a new scryer or someone who has had trouble with scrying, the last coat of paint is when you can add that glitter I recommended. Sprinkle a bit on the side that's going to be facing you when you work. This not only makes for a lovely presentation, but psychologically it gives your eyes something on which to catch. Why would that help? Well think about it—what do we associate darkness with? Sleep, closed eyes, night…but certainly not "seeing" something! So, you're using the glitter to provide that missing dimension. Like stars in the night sky on which people have wished, the glitter on your scrying mirror allows your mind to wander and helps open psychic windows. Again, this needs to dry completely.

I recommend putting one final coat of clear enamel over the giltter to make a finished surface. This is an optional step, but improves the longevity of your mirror. Additionally, you can tack or glue a lint free cloth at the top edge of the mirror. This is a way of keeping it clean between uses, and also acts as a mechanism through which you can spiritually open and close the mirror for use.

Once the mirror is complete, you can now bless and charge it in any way suited to your Path. Beyond this, there are some hints that should improve your success:

🜍 Keep the surface clean. You want a "pure" flow of energy when you're asking important questions.

ꙅ Each time you approach the mirror for insights, have your purpose in mind and keep your focus. Respect your tool as a partner in the process, but communicating with that "partner" helps a lot!

ꙅ If you find that your efforts at scrying suddenly hit a snag, or you're not getting any input or very slow, mixed signals, then it's probably time to recharge your tool. Like a battery, your mirror will need a regular flow of power to function at its best.

ꙅ Many books on scrying suggest that approaching your mirror during the full Moon yields better results.

ꙅ Burn incense to improve awareness while you're working with your mirror. This means that both you and your mirror use less energy overall.

ꙅ Finally, use candlelight as a cooperative tool. There's something about the gentle glow of candles that improves scrying efforts.

Care and Keeping of Your Scrying Mirror

While this tool is relatively inexpensive to make, the personal energy that goes into it is considerable. As a result, some practitioners prefer that no one but them use their personal mirrors. I happen to agree with this. While I'm not a selfish person, unless an individual is trained at working with spiritual archways, letting people tinker with your mirror is like leaving a door unlocked in your home. Additionally, tools tend to respond better when one person uses them regularly (it's a kind of attunement).

If you haven't chosen to add a cover to your mirror, then I'd suggest some type of padded storage area. An old box filled with shipping peanuts is one option. Foam is another. Whatever you choose, find a safe place in which to keep the mirror in between uses.

Chapter 24

Mortar and Pestle

Father, if we have the mortar without having the pestle as well, we shall have to get the pestle, so you had much better say nothing about it.

—Jacob and Wilhelm Grimm, *Household Tales*

In our discussions about herbs and incense we've brought up the usefulness of the mortar and pestle several times. Mortars are shaped like bowls and are typically made from stone, pottery, very hard woods, or marble. Think of a pestle like a baseball bat, one end of which grinds plant parts, and so on into uniform sizes.

History, Superstition, and Mythology

We see mortar and pestles similar to those we use today in 15th century paintings of apothecaries in Italy. However, there's no question that this tool is much older than that. In fact, it may be the oldest kitchen tool known to humankind. If we consider that the most important technology for everyday life in the ancient world was connected to preparing food, this possibility makes perfect sense. When early humans got tired of trying to grind various bits of seed or grain with their teeth, more than likely a rock was the first "pestle" with another rock's surface being the mortar.

The earliest grinding tools of this nature seem to date from the Paleolithic era. One was a slightly indented stone that would be handheld, with another stone for grinding. The small curve kept things from falling out.

Art has been another source for tracing the history of this implement. Egyptian tomb paintings from 1450 B.C.E. show two people working a mortar together. Another similar painting in Greece dated 500 B.C.E. shows a similar collaboration. And while these examples are simple, it's worthy to note that the larger mortar and pestle assemblies are the most likely forerunners of the mechanical grinding systems we have today!

A tool very similar to modern mortars and pestles was discovered in a Mexican archeological dig dating to 6,000 years ago (around the same time that people were starting to grow and utilize corn). This particular tool, called molcajete was made out of basalt, and was used exactly as a traditional mortar. They called the pestle tejolote. The two together were often employed in making salsa and mole, as well as for grinding herbs. Periodically a set has been found that was carved in the image of an animal, including pigs and bulls.

Superstition

In Thailand it is said that you should always have food in your mortar when you pound it. A woman who pounds an empty mortar will have her breasts stretch to the ground!

Meanwhile, north of the border Native Americans were carving mortars into bedrock as a place where they could effectively grind various nuts and other hard substances.

Mythology

Slavic lore tells us that Baba Yaga, a Guardian and Witch who protects the water of life, uses a mortar and pestle as the rudder to her flying broom! It's interesting that *baba* means "married woman," which may be part of the reason that a household tool became connected with this figure.

Later in history, the mortar and pestle became an integral part of pharmacies everywhere. Typically made of porcelain, this tool has become the most commonly used icon for pharmaceutical stores and companies.

Choosing a Mortar and Pestle

Commercially, these come in a variety of materials, and unless you're an adept craftsperson, it's going to be easier and less costly to simply buy the mortar you like. You can buy them readily over the Internet; however, I've found that the size of the pestle makes a huge difference in how comfortable this tool is in your hands, and therefore how effectively you can use it. So, go out to kitchen stores or department stores where you can try them out in person.

Granite is a chef's favorite because it's nonporous, features a good grinding surface, and is easily cleaned. On the down side, granite can splinter under pressure of pounding harder items. Look over the entire surface of the mortar and pestle for flaws. Deep cracks warn of potential breakage in the future.

Marble is another very adaptable choice. It doesn't absorb any odors (which is a huge plus if you're making a lot of aromatics). Like granite, it's easy to clean and maintain. Overall, the more you use a stone mortar, the more seasoned and responsive it becomes (akin to iron cookware).

Third in your list of options are ceramic or porcelain mortars and pestles. These do not stain or retain odor. They also don't show any wear and tear when you use them with acidic ingredients. The ceramic mortar was first made by the Wedgwood Company in the 1800s, because the wooden mortars, while popular, also presented health issues that the ceramics overcame. Porcelain makes a high-quality mortar, but can get costly.

Fourth is the basalt mortar that's favored in Spanish and Mexican cooking. The problem is that many mortars being sold as basalt are expensive, and some are fakes made from materials not recommended for cooking. If you're not planning to use your mortar for anything edible, that should be fine, but generally I issue caution in this choice.

Seasoning Lava Mortar and Pestles

If you're fortunate enough to find a real basalt mortar and pestle it requires seasoning before you use it. First wash it with water and scrub it using a Chore Boy–style scrub. Let it dry. Next grind some uncooked rice in the mortar. You'll notice the rice turns gray. Repeat the process of grinding fresh rice until it no longer looks gray when you're done. If you wish, you can now use kosher salt and pepper, likewise grinding this in the mortar. Rinse and dry before using. After this process, it is best to just rinse a basalt mortar, as dish soap often has perfumes that the stone can absorb (this would ruin the flavor of many foods).

A fifth option is called the Suribachi, a Japanese mortar and pestle. Traditionally, this is fashioned from earthenware. The exterior of the mortar is smooth, but internally it's textured to assist with grinding. The pestle is wooden, which keeps the interior ridges in the mortar from wearing away quickly.

Sixth, we come to iron. There's no question that with proper care a cast iron mortar and pestle will last a lifetime. Before using this, however, you should rinse it with water, dry with a paper towel, then spread a light coating of vegetable oil over all the iron surfaces. Note that these should never go in the dishwater, and must always be dried completely to avoid rust.

Finally, there's always wooden mortars and pestles. These are fine from a budget standpoint, but I do not recommend them for culinary activities. Wood is porous, meaning it will retain various aromas, oils, dusts, etc. From a health standpoint, this can be dangerous. So, if you opt for wood, seriously consider keeping it only for making nonedible magickal items.

Using This Tool

To use a mortar effectively, place small quantities of your chosen substance inside the bowl. Put the pestle on top and press down while also stirring to the right. As you do this, you'll notice aroma being released. That's because hand grinding actually releases oils and essences that commercial processors do not.

Now, don't forget to add the magical elements to your processing time. This is the perfect opportunity to saturate each of your ingredients with the energies most desired. Grind clockwise when fabricating "positive" energies. Grind counterclockwise when working on ingredients for decreasing or banishing. Burn candles or incense while you work, using colors and aromatics that match the overall production goal. Additionally, consider chanting or singing. Both of these raise energy and help you maintain your focus on the purpose of each component.

When you're done, if you're not going to use the component immediately, then store each item in a well-labeled, dark glass container with an air-tight top. I usually put a label inside too, in case the outer one comes off accidentally. Trust me when I say one ground-up seed can look a lot like another one! The reason for the glass container is to increase the item's longevity. Heat, light, and air all decrease the overall aroma and oils, especially in spices.

Rinse and dry your mortar and pestle before using it on another component. This will keep various oils and aromas from mingling, which in turn can also alter the magick you're hoping to create.

Chapter 25

Music and Sound

Sound when stretched is music.
Movement when stretched is dance.
Mind when stretched is meditation.
Life when stretched is celebration.

—Shri Shri Ravishankar Jee

To the great thinker Pythagoras, (sixth century B.C.E., Greece) our planetary system makes sounds akin to a harmonious chord as each plant moves through the spheres. This combined to make celestial music, the music of the Divine. Pythagoras also trusted in the healing power of music, by extension. And if you were to look at modern writings about sound therapy and sound magick, you'd find very similar outlooks. Sound is a vibration, and music is the universal language, so it only makes sense that Witches would utilize various sounds to augment their metaphysical efforts. The sound or music can communicate intention, even when words are wanting.

Sounding Off About History

Music developed in humans as a means of communication. The basic elements that create music really haven't changed since our forebears discovered them. It begins with sound and/or actions such as plucking on a taught string, banging objects together, humming, whistling, and blowing air over an opening or the surface of an item (such as grass). Because many of these sounds mirrored things in Nature, it allowed humans to communicate over distances without putting themselves in so much danger. Alternatively, tribes might make loud noises to scare away malicious spirits (not to mention wandering animals).

As society and culture grew, with it came more music—in many cases of a religious nature. There is no question that music reflected various shifts in human awareness, including our search for the Divine. One good example comes from Jewish history where the Israelites would dance, sing, and play music in processionals as they moved the Arc of the Covenant. In many settings it was felt that music rejoiced the heart of the gods, and acted as a bridge to communing with them.

The history of music and sound, and how it intertwines with spiritual experiences is a huge topic, not easily explored in a book of this nature. You could, in fact, write entire books on one instrument or song composition. What's important here is knowing that music and sound have long been integral to all manner of metaphysical methods, including meditation, ritual, and even mediumship. Music inspires the right/intuitive side of our minds, thereby allowing us to open inner doorways that we might not normally be able to access. They key is finding the sounds/music that inspire a spiritual release.

Sacred Sounds in Magick

Songs and clapping; chants and mantras; drums and digideroos. These types of sounds and so many others participate in our magick. I cannot imagine my pantry enchantments without the presence of my favorite Pagan CDs playing in the background, for example. And when that isn't playing, you'll probably find me humming my magick into each meal.

The beauty of many sounds is that you have what you need with you all the time—fingers for snapping, feet for stomping, and your voice for singing. Now, don't get worried if you're not the most rhythmic person, or the most adept vocalist. Really, your intention matters more than perfection here.

In particular, I'd like to explore the role of chanting and mantras to Kitchen Witchery, as I've found examples of these or similar vocalizations in a variety of folkways connected with the hearth and home. Consider the little ditties that women said over the butter churn as but one illustration. These served to keep a rhythm, but were also intended to be a charm that helped the butter set up properly. In effect, that's what chanting can do for us too—improve our focus and support the magick.

Chant

A chant is basically a rhythmic repetition of words, usually in a sing-song manner, and frequently rhymed. Rhyme helps with the mnemonic process so that the person's attention is wholly on an intention rather than remembering words—something very valuable to improving magick's manifestation.

Chanting appears in religious traditions around the world, including Native American, Buddhism, Islam, and Christian Psalms. This diversity speaks highly of the usefulness of this method.

So is there some trick to chanting? Not really, but step one is getting used to the sound of your voice. Read some of your favorite sacred materials out loud. Now, find a prayer or inspirational passage. Read it and listen to your voice so you know where to put emphasis. Next, start thinking about meaning and goals. Try it again. Keep your tone simple—you need not be loud, just clear and even-toned. If the piece has a natural rhythm (which many Pagan chants do), accent each line according to that rhythm.

To me, the biggest difference between speaking and chanting is the level of involvement. Instead of superficial words, your entire body vibrates with the energy you're creating—each sound bears a vibrational message. Maintain connected breaths, tone, and most of all stay committed to your purpose.

Mantra

Words have creative power. In the Vedas it says that speech embodies the human essence. All of what we think and become has a connection to what we say. So it is not surprising to see Hindu and Buddhist beliefs embracing the mantra as a necessary spiritual tool for human advancement.

Mantras are energy-based sounds. Part of that energy comes from the words spoken, the other part from personal intention (you can see pretty quickly here that mantras and chants have a lot in common). Not only does the recitation of the mantra create a vibration, but it also creates a thought wave from the practitioner. This consciousness, reaching out from the self, can not only communicate energy, but also gather information. In other words, mantras help a person achieve a heightened awareness where he or she can both express an intention and discern incoming energies. Doing so also changes the overall spiritual energies housed in a person's body—it aids in becoming the magick!

With this in mind, it's easy to understand why *mantra* means "to free the mind."

It's nearly impossible to describe the experience that occurs with effective utilization of a mantra. I could tell you how hot a fire feels, but until you feel it yourself that experience doesn't translate well. Mantras are like that. However, the most widely known and utilized mantra is simply "Om"—or "I am." This is an excellent place to start your adventure with mantras—a simple affirmation of self and Self.

Sit comfortably and breathe deeply. Repeat Om (or I am) in any way that feels right. You might speak quietly, sing, or whatever feels most comfortable to you. As you do, you may find that other sounds or words begin to flow of their own accord. This is very normal, and actually means you're on the right track. Nearly every mantra ever written came through meditation or intuitive "ah-ha" moments.

For me this moment happened when meditating with some friends at a lovely farmhouse. We had talked somewhat about mantras and meditation, but I really didn't expect anything to happen. Nonetheless, after several minutes, a series of words came into my mind unbidden. They were easy on my tongue, and I discovered later each was a real word in various languages. I believe I tapped a bit of my past-life experiences that day and received words reflecting some of my soul's memories.

I have used that mantra ever since along with a few others that have strong meanings to me. A mantra to which you have no connection also bears no transformative power. By the way, mantras are often used in combination with visualization. When healing, for example, a person might envision the part of his or her body that requires healing being bathed in light as he or she repeats the mantra. If you feel the need to use your imaginative energies, by all means do so!

One final note on mantras: At some point in your meditation you may find that the words simply fade. That too is perfectly normal. Mantras have a calming, quieting effect on the mind and body. As peace settles over you, it's natural to give way to silence. Silence is a unique "sound" of which we get all too little in this hectic world. So when your exercise brings that moment of stillness, enjoy it and listen. Listen to your heart, your breath, and Spirit.

Movement and Sound

A last note in the chapter on music and sound (pun intended) is the connection between sound, movement, and magick. If you've watched a ritual that includes a spiral dance, or sat back as dancers moved around a sacred fire to drumming, you know that there's an underlying hum to it all. It seems (to me) to be one of the most perfect ways to raise and direct energy. The sound speaks of your intent, your body moves with the intent, and the Goddess joins in as a dance partner.

So the next time you feel the urge to sing, hum, chant, or incant in your kitchen, do a little jig too! Pick up that wooden spoon, sing into it, and celebrate the magick that comes from your voice and vision working in harmony.

Chapter 26

Offerings and Libations

Of all the gods, Death only craves not gifts:
Nor sacrifice, nor yet drink-offering poured Avails;
no altars hath he, nor is soothed
By hymns of praise. From him alone of all
The powers of heaven Persuasion holds aloof Aeschylus.
                                        —Aeschylus (525–456 B.C.E.)

The word *sacrifice* comes from a term that translates as meaning "make sacred." This definition gives this writer pause to consider what that means in the greater scheme of things. While sacrifice and offerings are typically along the lines of gems, beverages, animals, and other valuables given to the Divine (in various ways), by extension, offering can be the good deeds we do for others. Service is a very real kind of offering, but I'm getting ahead of myself.

Generally speaking, offerings and libations have been used as a way of honoring, improving, or maintaining a person's or group's relationship with the Divine. This gift expresses faith, love, and sometimes acts as penance, usually in the hopes of gaining Divine favor.

Theology and History of Offerings

Nearly every society experienced some level of sacrifice and offering. Religiously speaking, while the methods have changed, many faiths still have offerings today. The reason for this varies, and the rituals by which the item is given to the Divine is likewise highly diversified. In reviewing global practices it seems that offerings:

ℑ Sustain the Divine, giving them power

ℑ Appease the Divine as a bargain (that is some favor is promised in return)

ℑ Please the Divine

ℑ Help the practitioner divorce from earthly needs

ℑ Turn away Divine wrath (which is visited on the sacrifice, such as an animal)

ℑ Support priests and priestesses (an economic base) when they had no other means of keeping up the sacred sites

ℑ Feed the poor and become a means of sharing blessings

Let's put this in the context of some specific religious traditions for more continuity. In Jewish tradition the word for sacrifice means to "come close to God." I think that's a lovely sentiment that certainly ties into the original meaning of "making sacred."

In any case, there were several different types of "acceptable" animal and vegetable offerings among the Jews, such as guilt offerings, sin offerings, peace offerings, burnt offerings, and meat and drink offerings.

The interesting part of the Jewish views here was that the leaders and teachers didn't want people depending too heavily on offerings. It seemed an "easy out," whereas living an honest, good life devoted to the Divine wasn't so simple! Those prophets were pretty wise folk. By the way, once the concept of animal sacrifice had been done away with, prayer and meditation were

200

regarded as suitable offerings! Considering how busy most people are these days, I'd have to agree that giving your time to the Divine in either of these ways can become a type of offering.

While it might seem deplorable to modern-minded folk, both animals and humans were often part of the offering process. We see the sacrifice of animals among the Greeks, Romans, Hebrews, and many African tribal belief systems (just to name a few). This often occurred as part of dedicating a Temple, when great leaders died (the person or animal then became an afterlife servant), and in the face of natural disaster to try and deter angry gods. The Aztec were perhaps the most prevalent in using human sacrifice. Each day at sunrise one such offering was made, and when the temple at Tenochtitlan was dedicated, apparently thousands of people were offered up. However, among the Egyptians it was forbidden, and in other systems certain creatures were taboo (such as the sacred cows of India).

Among the Carthaginians (an offshoot of Phoenicians) animal sacrifice was predominant. They even had laws specifying which animals could be used for specific types of offerings. An ox, ram, or lamb, for example, could be used as a burnt offering, peace, offering, or prayer offering along with a payment to the priest for his efforts. Birds were preferred as offerings to avoid disaster or for use in divinatory efforts. Note, however, that priests could not accept payment beyond what the law prescribed or they faced fines for doing so.

Offerings as a Magickal Tool

Both offerings and libations appear on the altar at various times of the year as our way of thanking Spirit and Earth for their gifts, or as a way of honoring a specific energy. While I do not believe the gods have need of such things, there is a very special magick in gratitude and giving that cannot be denied. Both seem to open energetic doors for blessings.

201

There's no question that the original reason for sacrifice was based in fear and superstition. However, the concept of balance is a powerful one, not to be undermined by humankind's early naivete. For example, when I have a serious financial need in my life and I've exhausted all resources, I will frequently look through personal items that have meaning to me. This item gets placed purposefully and mindfully on the "sales" altar. I confess, it is sometimes very hard to emotionally disconnect from "things," but, ultimately, remaining a co-creator in my destiny and a good provider to my family is more important. Typically within a few weeks of selling that item, money follows. Sometimes it's unexpected, other times it's from work already in progress. So, my offering is a tool, a component, a method of opening the path.

In terms of adding this tool into personal practices, the first question you should ask yourself is what the offering is for and what it represents. If the offering is a way of honoring a Deity, for example, the item chosen should be suited to that Deity. Most gods and goddesses have things they protect or regard as sacred. These are the kinds of things that might be suited to the altar for the purpose of worship. If an offering is being used to invite blessings, it should represent the kinds of things that you hope to receive. And if the offering is utilized as a means of trying to fix a problem or error, again, it should be suited to that task somehow. What happens to the offering, however, might vary. For example, sometimes the offering simply stays on the altar with the image of the Divine to whom its been given.

Food offerings can go outside to be shared with wild animals that then transport your prayers as they internalize them from the food. Offerings of jewelry might end up being gifted to someone who will understand the gesture and honor the energies therein. Money offerings may end up going to a suitable charity (one reflective of your goals). Leave your heart and mind open to the possibilities and listen when that little voice of the Divine guides.

Chapter 27

Oils

Why does pouring oil on the sea make it clear and calm? Is it for that the winds, slipping the smooth oil, have no force, nor cause any waves?

—Plutarch

There is no question that aromatic oils are a valuable part of a Kitchen Witch's tool kit. We can anoint with them, use them to scent candles and incense, dab them on lintels, rub them into various other magickal tools to inspire specific energy, and so much more. Better still, oils are something we can make easily at home. Before looking at that process and some more specific magickal applications, however, let's peek briefly at the amazing history of aromatic oils.

Oiling the Wheel of History

Throughout the world, oils were used in religious ritual. Priests and priestesses were among the first perfumers, being entrusted with the making and care of sacred oil. Egyptian priests in particular were known for their skills with fragrances by 2700 B.C.E. This was a good thing, considering the enormous amounts they used. For example, fragrant incense (scented with oils and herbs) was offered to the Sun god three times a day in Heliopolis alone. Oil was also very important to mummification, and to the healing arts.

When Cleopatra ascended the throne, she was already skilled in the art of perfume. She had the sails of her royal barge soaked in lily oil when first meeting Marc Anthony. The scent was so strong that much later in history Shakespeare described even the winds as being lovesick.

The Hebrews took a cue from the Egyptians and adapted the art of perfumery to their own religious needs. There are 188 references to oils in the Bible. In particular we read in Exodus 30:22-25:

> Moreover, the Lord spoke unto Moses saying: Take thou also unto thee principal spices of pure myrrh…of sweet cinnamon…of sweet calamus…of cassia…and of olive…and thou shalt make it an oil of holy ointment, an ointment compound after the art of the apothecary: it shall be an holy anointing oil.

Historians believe this passage dates to approximatly 1446 B.C., at the time of the exodus from Egypt.

Hindus, Buddhists, and Muslims also used a wide variety of aromatics in worship and meditation. In fact, many continue to do so. As with many religious implements, it wasn't long before people started wanting aromatic oils for personal use. They were extraordinarily expensive, so of course only the most affluent could afford this luxury. The trade routes from the Mediterranean brought a wide variety of essentials, some being called perfume. Oddly, though, this perfume wasn't always what we think of, but oil-scented incense too (*perfume* means "through smoke"). The clever merchants quickly realized the lore of the plants associated with each stocked oil only made the items more valuable. The greater magickal power it offered, the better!

Romans in particular seemed enamored of essential oils. Emperor Nero had pipes hidden in the walls of his home so as to spray perfume on his guests.

When Christianity arrived on the scene we found Mary Magdalene anointing Jesus' feet at the Last Supper. By the time of Constantine, anointing became part of the crowning of kings. And in the Middle Ages we find a flourishing oil trade following the same routes as merchants had in 1700 B.C.E.! As a reflection of the popularity of scented oils, Queen Elizabeth I had a team of floral distillers on call.

Once bathing became more of a ritual, oils were used to clean people. The oil was massaged in, then scraped off. Additionally, people readily carried oiled sachets to repel bugs and sickness—patchouli, lavender, cloves, ambergris, orris, and rosemary being used for that function quite popularly.

Moving into modern day, we continue to use oil in a wide variety of ways from cooking to the automotive industry, and of course in our magick.

Making Basic Aromatic Oils

The easiest way to make homemade aromatic oil begins with three parts good quality oil (I use virgin olive or almond), to which you add one part dry aromatic matter (such as a spice), or two parts fresh aromatic matter (such as flower petals).

Wrap the aromatic matter in cheesecloth. Put the oil in a non-aluminum pan and warm it. Steep the cheesecloth therein over a very low heat until you get the amount of scent desired. Note that you can add more aromatic if it's not strong enough after about 30 minutes of simmering. If it's too strong, simply add more oil. Gently squeeze the aromatic matter when you remove it from the oil. Cool, then store in a dark, airtight container. If the oil ever takes on a cloudy appearance, throw it out and make a fresh batch. This means the oil has turned, and with it the magick.

Generally speaking, I recommend making one-scent oils, then blending from those for other effects. My reason for this is that aromatics decoct at different rates, and some are more sensitive to heat than others. You want to be able to get the best scent possible, which means treating the chosen aromatic individually, tending to its unique nature when making the oil. Label your bottles, then mix and match as you wish.

Don't forget the magickal part of the process while you work. You can chant, sing, add crystals to the oil vials that match your goals, bless the oil, and/or charge it when you're done. Just remember to note your intentions on the oil's label for future use.

Magickal Applications

One very popular use for aromatic oils among magickal practitioners is that of "dressing" ritual and spell candles. The idea is to add the energies of the aromatic oil to the candle, then light the candle to activate that energy. This can act as subtle aromatherapy above and beyond the mundane advantage of making an area smell nice.

Other applications for your oils include:

ᔕ Bath: Surround your aura with the aromatics you need to improve overall well-being. Light a candle and slip into a warm, luxurious magickal bath. This is also a very nice way to prepare for special rituals. If you're a shower person, dab some oil on a scrap of cloth and hang it from the shower to release the aroma.

☾ Meditation: Pick out an aroma that helps you center and focus. Place a little on your pulse points, chakaras, and Third Eye before settling in to meditate. Make note of how different scents affect your meditation efforts.

☾ Massage: Blend together some relaxing oils like lavender and vanilla for wonderful massage oils that literally rub you the right way. The massage works the energies of the oils directly into the skin. Caution: Always try a little oil on a very small spot first to ensure there's no allergic reactions.

☾ Lightbulbs: When your home is a little stressful, take some calming oils and put a drop on lightbulbs so you can "turn on" the magick therein.

☾ Pet collars: Soak your pet's collars in a solution of water, fennel oil, pennyroyal oil, and other protective choices that also ward off fleas!

☾ Ointments: Add some of your specially made oil to an unscented cream. This is really nice if you like to have aromatics with you on the road but don't want to worry about having oils leak onto your ritual wardrobe. Spot test first to make sure you don't have an allergic reaction.

Finally, speaking of ritual, let's not forget the sacred space. Make four Elemental oils (Earth, Air, Fire, Water) and use these to anoint the Four Quarters of your sacred space. You can get information on the Elemental associations of various aromatics in books such as my *Floral Grimoire* (Citadel Press, 2001) and other magickal herbals.

Chapter 28

Pentacles and Pentagrams

Go, and catch a falling star,
Get with child a mandrake root,
Tell me, where all past years are,
Or who cleft the devil's foot,
Teach me to her mermaids singing,
Or to keep off envy's stinging,
And find what wind
Serves to advance an honest mind.

—John Donne

By definition, a pentagram is a five-pointed star. It comes from the Greek word *pente*, meaning "five" and *gram* meaning "to write." By comparison, the pentacle is an upright pentagram within a circle. In upright form, the pentacle and pentagram are among the most utilized symbols in varying religious traditions.

Pointing the Way to the Pentagram

A five-pointed star was a very common design in a variety of settings including China, India, and Latin America. Some of the earliest pentagrams date back to about 4000 B.C.E. in the region of Palestine. Archaeological digs also uncovered Mesopotamian pentagrams in 3500 B.C.E., where they represented the ruling power, and several uses of pentagrams in Sumeria dating to 2700 B.C.E. There is some argument as to what the Sumerian pentagram meant, but most historians feel it was a cosmic symbol connecting all of creation to the heavens. Primarily, it was used on pottery designs and may have also been a sigil for good health. The pentagram may also have represented the five planets visible to the naked eye.

By 400 B.C.E. Pythagoreans were using a pentagram in their signature line as a way of identifying each other. The common explanation of the pentagrams meaning to Pythagoreans was that of the human microcosm, with arms stretched out to the circle, which is infinite.

Meanwhile in other settings, a five-pointed star honored the Queen of Heaven, such as Ishtar or Venus. In Hebrew tradition, the pentacle was among the Seven Seals, and it was inscribed on King Solomon's seal, each point representing one of the five books of the Torah.

Come the Christian era the pentagram symbolized the five wounds of Christ. Constantine began using it as a personal seal and protective amulet. It wasn't until the Middle Ages that the pentagram took on negative connotations, even though it was still:

- appearing on doors in Norse regions to protect those within
- a symbol of the five knightly virtues of generosity, courtesy, chastity, chivalry, and piety
- being used as a symbol of truth and an amulet against demons.
- used in esoteric belief systems including alchemy and high magick
- Leonardo da Vinci used it as part of an illustration showing man's relationship to the universe.

It's worth noting, however, that the negativity was mostly directed toward the inverted pentacle. The first appearance of this item came from inquisition interrogations, so the truth of how it was used (if at all during that time) is questionable.

In modern times, Rosicrucians use a pentagram in mystical rituals. Here it symbolizes earth, matter, and stability. The Masons also use the pentagram as a symbol of the five points of fellowship. Ritual magicians use the symbol as a means to bridge the gap between worlds and come into closer fellowship with the Divine. Jewish Cabbalists have the pentagram as a representative of the five upper sephiroth on the Tree of Life, each of which is a fundamental force—justice, mercy, wisdom, understanding, and transcendence.

The Masons use the five-pointed Seal of Solomon as part of their symbolic elements. Similarly, the Eastern Star, the women's branch of the Masons, uses a five-pointed star. Each point here represents a different admired woman in the Bible.

Finally, Wiccans have adopted the pentacle as a sacred symbol, often interpreted to represent the five Elements of Earth,

Air, Fire, Water, and Spirit. Sometimes the symbol appears on altars, other times it's drawn as part of blessings, anointings, and casting Circles. Pentagrams and pentacles regularly appear as part of ritual wear, painted or embroidered on robes, burnt into wooden candle holders, and patterned on jewelry.

Making a Pentagram

In my travels I've seen a rich variety of homemade pentagrams and pentacles. Some were knit or tatted, others were quilted, some were elaborately painted and others still were done in stained glass. Now, being that I have rather poor eyesight, I usually lean toward projects that aren't quite so intricate. Two in particular that don't take long and lend themselves nicely to a fast afternoon project with children are a candle pentagram and a twig pentagram.

For the candle project you'll need five self-enclosed candles of the same size in the colors white, blue or purple, brown or green, red or orange, and yellow. I suggest using votive-sized or just a little larger as the finished product is much easier to handle that way. If you're using large candles, you will want to assemble this where you're going to use it. You'll also need double-sided tape.

Beginning with the white candle, which will be the top point of your pentagram, place two pieces of double sided tape on the outside of the container to the left and right. On the right side you can now connect the yellow candle (for Air), and on the left connect the brown candle (Earth). On the yellow candleholder place another piece of the tape on the inside of the container. Do likewise on the inside of the brown candle container. Put the Fire candle adjacent to the Air and again put a piece of double-sided tape on the inside of the container. Finally, put the Water candle in place. Push gently on the candles so the tape holds. This now is a visually pleasing pentagram that you can light as you invoke the Elements and the Deity. By the way, I put Spirit at the top with the Elements arranged clockwise in the order most Witches invoke them (Air, Fire, Water, Earth). If your tradition invokes differently, you may wish to change the order accordingly.

The twig pentagram requires five equal-length sticks about a quarter inch in diameter and sturdy twine. If you are going to want a pentacle, you'll also need some grapevine. Lay two twigs before you to form the upward point consisting of two twigs touching at the top. On top of this lay the third, which will be the top cross bar of the pentacle. Use twine to bind the place where the bar piece crosses the other two sticks. Now take the final two sticks and bind them in the center so they make an X. Lay this so that two ends of the X touch the two ends of the cross bar. The top portion of these last two twigs will cross the two foundational twigs that make your upper point. Bind them at those two junctures again with the string.

To make this sturdier, you can now use wood glue to secure the bound points. I also like to add colored yarn at each of the points and symbolic objects for a nicely finished item. What's nice about this is that you can change what you put on the twigs as the Wheel of the Year changes. Or Kitchen Witches might put herbs on their pentagram and hang it in the kitchen!

If you want a pentacle, all you need to is surround the star with the grapevine, attaching it at the five points. I use florist wire for this purpose and add a loop for hanging at the same time.

213

Chapter 29

Potions

It's actually the spirit helping the spirit; it is the doctor, the bed, the potion.

—Franz Grillparzer

What's bubbling in your cauldron or cup? Is it an elixir of energy, a brew of bounty, or a potion of prosperity? It might be a draught of love, an infusion of insight, or a concoction for cleansing! Or more modernly maybe you're using Bach's flower essences instead. In any case, potions are among the most popular of "low magicks" used in the Witch's kit.

Pouring Over History

It's nearly impossible to talk about Witch's potions without getting knee deep into the history of beverages in general and their religious uses around the world. Exactly who made brews and potions, what was in the potion, and how it got used varied a lot from culture to culture and era to era. For example, we know that the ancient Peruvians and Greeks gave their seers some type of alcoholic potion to aid with divinatory effects. One assumes these beverages had some type of mind-altering effect to open the seer as a doorway to the Divine.

What makes the exploration even more difficult is that nearly every type of potion ever made by a cunning person seems to have a very diversified and rich history all its own. Love potions are an excellent example, having documentation reaching as far back as 2400 B.C.E. in Egypt, and other very early examples in Persia and China. Come the time of Louis XVI, making love potions had become an art, one in which Catherine LaVoisin was well versed. She was continually making passion-inspiring concoctions for the King's mistresses with a variety of herbs including cinnamon, nutmeg, rose, and fennel. Other love potions of the same period used ginseng, yarrow, jasmine, parsley, and daffodil. Each magician based his or her compounds on mythical, alchemical, and magickal associations along with governing Deities, even as we do today.

Besides matters of the heart, potions were very popular in healing. If a healer wanted an ailment to wane, he or she might prepare a potion during the waning Moon, mingling in a variety of invocations as they worked. In reading the ingredient list for some of these cures, it would seem that the potion was worse than the malady, such as the use of toads in potions for heart problems. However, we know today that toad skin contains a substance similar to digitalis, meaning it might have actually helped the patient!

Sadly, many magickal brews were not healthy or safe. It is one of the reasons that laws were established regarding poisons. There were a lot of proverbial money-changers looking to take advantage of those willing to pay large sums for miracles. Afterward they'd skip town, leaving a wake of sick, or even dead, people.

On the other side of this equation was the well-intended Witch who was following a recipe and found out the hard way it wasn't helpful.

This is a very important point to remember as you read potion recipes in any historical text. Before trying such a thing, always check the ingredients against modern scientific and medical texts to ensure that anything you plan to consume is wholly safe. In particular with plants, double check the botanical designations as one species in the same genus can cure, while another can kill. The best rule is if you're not absolutely sure, just don't go there.

Back to health, a book called the *Secrets of Wines* from the 1700s talks about curatives based in brandy. Among the recipes we find a maternity anise and a heart cordial, both of which have stronger magickal associations. This is also a very good illustration of how common beverages participated in the history of Witch's potions.

Speaking of beverages, sometimes they were consumed unaltered, the practitioner trusting in blessing for the desired goal. One example of this comes from Peru where a specially prepared beverage (Haomas) would be lifted in a cup with an invocation. We read in the Yasha liturgy, "I claim to thee, O'yellow one for inspiration, for strength, for vigor." While this beverage was already regarded as sacred, this gesture to the heavens was intended to unlock the potion's benefits to the drinker—akin to a toast or premeal prayer today.

Here are some more examples of how beverages were used as magickal potions in their own rite:

- Mead was poured on water as a charm to ensure safe sailing (Greece).
- Apple trees received offerings of cider to inspire a good harvest (Europe).

- ᕱ Angelica steeped in vinegar and consumed turns away negative influences (Anglo-Saxon).

- ᕱ Sprinkling water from a sacred well during draught will bring the rains (Welsh).

- ᕱ The surface of mead sometimes became a scrying implement (Scandanavia).

- ᕱ Drinking mead on one's honeymoon brings fertility (Celtic).

- ᕱ Wine and beer were regularly offered to gods and goddesses (Egypt).

It's easy to see here that there are a lot of good ideas from which the clever pantry sorcerer can adapt new potions, or old ones with a modern twist.

Potions and Notions: Making Your Witch's Brew

Before going further, I'd like to make it clear that I feel anything, including water, can become a potion if you bless and charge it with the proper focus and will. This awareness is important to the time-challenged Kitchen Witch. For example, maybe you'd like to offer a prayer over orange juice for improved health instead of trying to whip up a potion when you're under the weather!

I approach potion making in a similar manner as amulets. First I choose an astrologically supportive time frame within which to make the brew. This isn't a necessary step, but it does lend a little extra symbolic "oomph" to your crafting process. For example, make the potion at noon if it's focused on a goal associated with the Fire Element (energy, strength, leadership, and so on). Or make the potion when the Moon is full to stimulate more intuitive Water energies therein.

218

Second, I consider components. A primary consideration in components is whether this is a potion for consumption, libation, or one that will be used as a prop in a spell or ritual. If the former, obviously it's important to choose those ingredients that are drinkable. It helps if the potion tastes good, too. The negativity of a scrunched up face from a nasty tasting brew doesn't support the internalization and manifestation process.

Third, have a little fun. Take a look at each step of the process for your potion and see what extra meaning you can bring to it. Here are some ideas to get you started:

- Stir the potion clockwise for encouraging specific energies (counterclockwise to reverse specific energies as in banishing).
- Use non-aluminum pots. There's something about aluminum that seems to shift magickal energies. The potion will also taste better.
- Create a potion brewing kit (spoon, pot, and measurer) that you only use for spiritual purposes.

Fourth, use clever glass bottles for storing your potions. I've found some of the most wonderful bottles at secondhand shops and flea markets—some shaped like a goddess, some like animals, and some made from colored glass that support my goals. I do recommend dark, airtight containers to improve the overall longevity of your potions. I also recommend good labels complete with intention and ingredient lists. This avoids a lot of potential problems with allergies if you share the potions with others.

Chapter 30

Prayer and Meditation Beads

Prayer is the fair and radiant daughter of all the human virtues, the arch connecting heaven and earth, the sweet companion that is alike the lion and the dove; and prayer will give you the key of heaven. As pure and as bold as innocence, as strong as all things are that are entire and single, this fair and invincible queen rests on the material world; she has taken possession of it; for, like the sun, she casts about it a sphere of light.

—Honoré De Balzac

While one might associate prayer beads more strongly with Catholicism or Eastern esoteric traditions, there's been several adaptations of this idea in the Neo-Pagan community well worth considering. One was a lovely gift I received from a friend as a housewarming gift. It was made from clay, each bead of which looked like a flower, the central piece was a simple goddess image, and it was anointed with blessing oil.

To understand the various potentials for our prayer beads, lets first look at how other belief systems have utilized them.

Stringing Together History

In both Catholicism and Buddhism, prayer beads are a part of devotion and act as a meditative, focusing tool. By repeating a prayer or mantra a certain number of times, the practitioner's mind turns inward and upward. The beads come in a wide variety of mediums ranging from berries and wood to precious stones and metals.

Prayer beads were a rather natural outgrowth of various religious requirements. We can consider Abbot Paul (341 C.E.) who used pebbles to count his daily prayers, moving one out of his lap as the words were recited to ensure completion. Around the eigth century C.E., Christians were given prescriptions for the number of prayers they had to say for forgiveness of specific sins. It is said that Countess Godiva donated her set of gemstone prayer beads upon her death to the image of Mary.

Later in history certain military orders such as the Knights of St. John used beads as a sign of membership. Where the beads were worn and what they could be made out of differed from order to order. Some monks were prohibited, for example, from wearing amber beads (presumably because that was ostentatious).

As the popularity of prayer beads increased in the Western world, they became a valued item for gift-giving. If someone of import once had worn or blessed the beads, all the better. At this juncture beads were still being strung on cord with a larger bead or other marker separating sets of beads (often 10). The traditional Rosary has 168 to 169 beads (150 for Hail Mary prayers, 15 for Our Father prayers, and several others for introductory phrases).

Moving to the Far East, we find many other examples of such tools. In India, for example, we discover 108 wooden beads that correspond to the names of Vishnu and invocations to Shiva. These are sometimes given to children during coming of age rituals. Buddhists likewise bear 108 beads for prayers and mantras made of coral, gems, or metals. These can be found in China, Tibet, and Japan, often with a token at the end of the strand such as the word *Om*, which is both an affirmation and an invocation.

Moslem custom is that of using 100 prayer beads, at least one of which represents the unknown name of Allah. These appeared as early as the ninth century. Travelers to Mecca bring their beads with them to be blessed, and many of the sets are made from the clay in this region to ensure their sanctity.

Making Prayer and Meditation Beads

Making floral beads is a very old custom, probably linked into the perfuming industry (perhaps as a way of using leftovers effectively). We know that during the Middle Ages such items were kept in drawers or carried as wards against plague, or simply to make people who bathed infrequently smell better!

The first question in your bead making is simply: For what purpose are you designing these items? Will they become an amuletic gift for friends, blessed for a purpose? Will they become part of a necklace or bracelet to aid in personal focus?

While answering this won't affect the design of the bead much, it will affect your choice of flower petals, and possibly your working times. Traditionally, roses are used, but I've had success with several other flowers, including magnolias and lilac. So consider the symbolism of various flowers, then choose one according to your goals. If you wish to add timing as a component, think about whether making the beads during the day (Sun, god, vitality) or night (intuition, Moon, psychism, dreams) is better for your goal. You could also wait until an astrologically supportive time frame, if practicable.

Step two is obtaining a fairly good quantity of petals. To give you an idea, about two good handfuls of rose petals yield about 24 beads slighty smaller than a quarter. The better the flower's aroma, and the brighter its colors, the better the results seem to be. However, please make sure the flowers are organic—anything that's been treated will ruin your efforts.

Next, clean off the flowers. Do not use the white base of petals, and avoid any green parts. Dice these up finely in a food processor. Transfer this material to an iron pan and cover with water. Simmer the petals. Be patient! If you turn the heat up too high, you'll end up with bad-smelling beads. Simmer for one hour, cool completely, then repeat.

Now it's time to drain off as much water as possible. You can use this liquid in anything that calls for floral water! Put it in the refrigerator for up to a week for proper use.

Once the petals have been squeezed out, shape them into a ball or square twice the size you want (a circle has stronger Water-Goddess-oriented energy, while a square is more Earth-God oriented). There's typically about 50 percent shrinkage as they dry. If 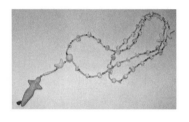 you'd like the beads to be more aromatic, you can add a drop or two of essential oil at this stage.

If you're going to string the bead on anything, this is the time when you have to create the hole. You can pierce the bead with a pin or wire, then put them on a surface to continue drying. It's very important that the beads have good exposure to air. One easy solution to this is to pin them to a corkboard. Over the next several days (at least four) turn the beads regularly to make sure they don't stick to the wire or pin.

When finished you can varnish them, but unless they get wet they're pretty durable as is. Some people add oris root to the cooking process as a fixative. In any case, until you're ready to use them keep them in an airtight container away from unpleasant aromas as they can absorb other scents. One neat trick is to put a cotton ball soaked in aromatic oil with the beads in storage. This improves the scent of your beads and keeps them fresh for whenever you want to use them.

Chapter 31

Staffs and Wands

She, crowned with olive green, came softly sliding
Down through the turning sphere,
His ready harbinger,
With turtle wing the amorous clouds dividing,
And waving wide her myrtle wand,
She strikes a universal peace through sea and land.

—John Milton

Sticks were among humankind's first tools—the first extension of self into the world. It increased the ways in which people could interact with their environment, from helping an elder to walk to fighting off an enemy. With that in mind, it is not surprising that sticks became part of magick in a variety of ways. As has become a mantra in this book, if something was used every day by enough people, it was likely to end up in religion, too.

For Witches, wands typically symbolize the Element of Fire (South), and the ultimate Male aspect. In some cases, however, where the idea of a talking stick has been borrowed from Native American customs, that wand might more rightly represent Air (communication/East). In the construct of a ritual space, wands often become part of invoking the Watchtowers and drawing various sigils in the air for protection.

Pointing Toward History

We can look to a great many cultures for examples of using a wand or staff in ritual and religion. Greek and Roman customs, however, seemed to rally around this symbol. Roman diviners

used special staffs as part of divinatory rites in several ways, for example. This includes drawing a circle on the ground or in the air, and watching the movement of animals or birds through that area afterward. Greek mythology is also dotted with wands and rods, including Mercury's sleep-producing wand.

Perhaps the most famous wand/staff is the Caduceus. Heralded as the legendary staff of the God of Medicine, Aesculapius, and the rod of Hermes, this staff was topped with wings intertwined by two snakes. Myths tell us that Hermes once threw his magick wand at two fighting snakes and when they became entangled, they were attached permanently. It was later Greek and Roman artists who added the wings. In any case, this staff was present each time Mercury and Hermes delivered a message to the gods. More mundanely, staffs wound with simple two white ribbons represented the authority of whatever herald held the item. This gives us pause to think about the authority with which we wield our own magick.

This isn't the first instance of such a staff in history. It's very likely that a Babylonian god named Ningizzida (who happened to carry a rod with snakes as early as 4000 B.C.E.) was first dibs, followed by the Hittites who had coins with a snake-staff on them neatly stationed between Divine images. There may also be ties to Cabbalistic traditions in that much of the symbolism of the Caduceus mimics the Tree of Life. This connection likely comes through Moses. Between using his rod in the court of the Pharoah to using it to yield water from a rock, there was a lot of power in that tool!

Our history certainly doesn't stop there. In Tacitus writings we find mention of German augury with small twigs from fruit-bearing tree branches. With a prayer to Odin, these were tossed akin to runes on a white cloth. Another person in a position of authority (such as a priest) would offer another prayer by looking to the sky and pick up one twig. The markings on that twig were regarded as the answer. A far simpler, yes-no type system from the same region shaved one side of a twig clean of its bark. If the twig landed white side up, it was a positive answer.

Making a Simple Wand or Staff

If you look at the Tarot, you'll see the Magician with one hand held upward, a wand therein. As if in invocation, the magician is one with his or her tools, and recognizes them as a conductor of the will and focus. It is as if, in that moment, the Magus is wholly in accord with Self and Godself. Fear has gone the way of confidence, and his or her tools are unlocking all manner of possibilities. In the traditional depiction of this card, the wand connects the practitioner to the "as above, so below" axiom, and helps us bridge the gap between realities. Effectively, the wand and staff becomes a magician's pointer on the chalkboard of the universe, directing the path of energy. With this in mind, exactly how you go about making your wand or staff, and with what basic materials, should be a carefully considered endeavor.

Some say that the customary size of a wand is the length measured from the tip of the middle finger of your strong hand, to the elbow. That size accentuates it as an extension of Self. However, if you don't find you're comfortable with that size, don't sweat it. It's most important that it feel right in your hands. Staffs are similar in that they typically are head height, but again should be of a weight and width that's comfortable.

A lot of practitioners like to work in wood. If you prefer this medium, get to know what each wood symbolizes magickally. For example, willow was often used in magick because it's pliable (magick is to bend and change!). Willow has healing attributes so it might well be used to make a staff or wand that will be used in magick "supporting" self, others, and even your community. Rowan supports lunar magick because

228

its leaves have 13 sections, and oak provides strength and surety because it is a very hard wood.

Now, unique circumstances do change the attributes in any piece of found wood. A lightning strike provides Air/Fire energies. Soaking over the winter in snow creates a strong Water-oriented staff. The latter is what I own (and the water soaking neatly removed the bark with very little difficulty). To that foundation I added a leather hand-hold, crystals given to me by readers (held in by wood glue to which I added some herbs), and a top point made from a Herkimer. Periodically I treat it with lemon oil to keep the wood from drying and cracking but other than that making the wand really wasn't time consuming.

Wands and staffs can certainly be made from other things. Go to the hardware store and get copper or glass rods, for example. Other decorative medium include feathers, beads, charms (such as those for bracelets), carvings, paintings, and so on. No matter your choice, please keep in mind that the medium and function should match both mundanely and magickally. To illustrate: if you travel a lot it's far more pragmatic to make a small wand with a protective cover that can go in your checked luggage.

Using the Wand and Staff

When a practitioner draws a sacred Circle with either of these tools it marks the boundary between "world" and "not world." In this setting, think of the implement as your means of determining your boundaries and holding them firm. As with any magickal method, it's important to keep your focus. Imagine a bright beam of light pouring from the end or tip of your wand/staff and drawing that outline, which is also a pattern of your intention and will. Additionally, a wand might be held up during ritual invocations (even as the Magician in the Tarot), bridging the gap between the worlds.

229

Another use for your wands (but one for which you need to fashion them differently) is in divination. The Saxons, for example, used a seven-rod system made from three short pieces of wood and four long pieces. One of the four long rods had special decorations and was placed along the ground on a North-South axis. The diviner held the remaining rods and focused on a question. Slowly, they would allow all but one rod fall to the ground above the North-South indicator. Any rod that connected with the indicator portended a no answer at that time. Similarly, if any of the rods touched each other, it was a non-answer. However, if all the rods pointed toward the indicator, the question could be solved with sound reasoning. If the rods

were parallel to the indicator, fate's hand was busily at work. A majority of the rods in the Eastern Quarter revealed a positive outcome, while, in the Western Quarter, a negative outcome.

A closely related system that offers greater interpretive value is one called the Druid rods. These appear to have modern origins, but are based in Druidical geomantic symbolism. Druid rods should be designed from the wood of fruit-bearing trees. Symbolically, this provides fertile energy with which to work. However, being that we want to keep things inexpensive, how about Popsicle sticks instead?

Paint each of four sticks with two circles on one side toward each end of the stick, and one circle on the other side in the middle. This creates 16 possible patterns. Now, just as the Saxons did, hold these in your hand and think of your question. Toss them on a cloth and straighten them out parallel to you (the one that lands closest to you is the bottom pattern).

230

Pattern Value

Pattern	Value
*	A path laid before you. Possible travel or opportunity.
* * *	Movement; action.
* * * * *	A new start. Be aware and alert. Keep your duties wisely balanced. Trust yourself.
* * * * *	Nurturing, insight, and improved relationships.
* * * * * *	Luck, victory, blessings. Karmic return threefold.
* * * *	God. Strength, leadership, and the necessity to harness the masculine energies within.
* * * * * * *	Gains, advancement, improvement, especially with money.

231

* * * * *	Obstacles. A closed door. Life on hold. Holding back positive action. Doubts.
* * * * * * *	Sadness. No hope. Unexpected loss; disappointment.
* * * * *	Decline or setback. Prepare bravely to meet adversity.
* * * * * * *	Unity, love, kinship, or friendship. Beneficial unions.
* * * * * * *	Technical troubles. Conflict and misunderstanding.
* * * * * *	Be patient and tenacious. Moderation in all things.

``
    *
  *   *
  *   *
  *   *
``
	A joyful bit of serendipity or success

``
    *
  *   *
  *   *
``
	Too much emotion and not enough logic.

``
    *
 	
  *   *
  *   *
  *   *
``
	In the Tarot this corresponds to the Sun—that is all good things. Carpe diem and find fulfillment.

``
  *   *
  *   *
  *   *
  *   *
``
	Listen to the people in and around your life.

An alternative way to cast the rods is tossing them nine successive times, then interpret the patterns by adding the significance of numerology. The first pattern represents the individual in the question. The second represents matters requiring discretion, especially in relationships. Pattern three equates to communication—your ability to express yourself effectively and how this influences the current question. Pattern four illustrates your ability to reason and act. Fifth speaks of liberation—what you need to be free from, or of what you must let go. The sixth pattern pertains to your home and personal duty. The seventh is focused on spiritual pursuits. Pattern eight correlates to money matters and your dreams vs. reality. The ninth symbol represents your ability to give and receive love. This last pattern may alternatively be read as the "outcome" to your question.

Chapter 32

Statuaries

Nobody, I think, ought to read poetry, or look at pictures or statues, who cannot find a great deal more in them than the poet or artist has actually expressed. Their highest merit is suggestiveness.
—Nathaniel Hawthorne

If you were to visit my home, you'd discover statues of Kwan Yin, Shiva, Lakshmi, Ganesha, and Bast in various locations, most on the altar. Are these necessary for worship? Not really, but statues give a face and shape to the Divine to which we can relate. Indeed, statues dating back to prehistoric times of various forces imply that there's a psychological need in humans to illustrate God, or at least our image of that Being. Somehow, so doing makes the connection more real, more understandable, more in the human domain. Effectively, modern Neo-Pagans are simply following in the path of our ancestors in this regard.

Carving Out History

I honestly would need an entire encyclopedia to share with you the places and ways in which statuary participated in religious rites around the world. Universally, statues were part of temples, were included in worship, sometimes had a role in divination, and eventually found their way into the home for family practices.

Let's look at Egypt. Wherever one looked, statues decorated the great places of this country. Starting around 1600 B.C.E. three-dimensional portraits of Ra, Osiris, Horus, and other divine figures became very noticeable. They stood alongside the face of the prevailing Pharaoh, who was also considered divine. Similar customs were evidenced even earlier than this in Assyro-Babylonian regions where statues date back to 2500 B.C.E. And wherever these larger-than-life pieces appeared, you could be fairly certain some type of religious activity would follow.

Perhaps the most ardent and detailed in statuary arts were the Greeks and Romans. The mythology of classical Greece and Rome was incredibly rich, and the arts were likewise enriched by that social foundation. Take, for example, the carved image of Ganymede with an eagle, complete with detailed wings, gently carved muscles, and a sense of life and movement in the stone. This piece dates to about 600 B.C.E. Thus was the cupbearer immortalized among humans in an image that inspires to this day.

An interesting note in the Greek histories is that certain Divine figurines were used for an odd form of divination. A person would go to a temple and whisper his or her question in the ear of a god. The person would then plug their ears and return outside. Releasing the ears, the first words heard thereafter were said to be the "answer" sought. This practice had some similarities to the custom of sleeping at the feet of a statue for a set number of days in the hopes of receiving a Divine-inspired dream.

In terms of home observances, we have an excellent example of this from Chinese tradition. Here, many kitchens have a statue of the Kitchen God, who is also the keeper of the family's moral fiber. According to lore, the Kitchen God reports to heaven once a year (23rd day of the last month on the Chinese Lunar calender). At this time, he tells what the family has done. In order to make sure this Being says only good things, the family gives him lotus root candy paste, typically placed on the lips of the statue.

Similarly, in Korea, house statuary was (and often still is) common. One figure represented the master god, who protected the house and the head of the family. A goddess figure was kept near the hearth to protect the wife of the house. Other Deities protected the gates and even the toilet, each of which had specific rituals of appeasement.

Rome is another place where household guardians were well defined and displayed. These were called the Lares, and each had a name and a place to occupy. First is the Lares Loci, who we would consider the spirit of the house itself and the land it occupies. This guardian was represented by a serpent. Second was the Genius, or house father, accompanied by the Di Penates, who occupy the storeroom (a very essential part of any home!). The Penates often received offerings of food and drink so that the hearth and home would always be filled with both.

237

If the house were not already crowded with spiritual guests, there was also the Manes to consider—the spirits of ancestors who protect the family. And let's not forget the door guardian, Foculus, hinge spirit Cardea, Vesta the goddess of the hearth, and even Deverra, whose dominion was the household broom! Seriously, there seemed to be a Lares for every occasion and space including marriage, sex, nourishment, and pregnancy! While we need not get this in depth, it's certainly an interesting snapshot in history of a time when the gods were welcome and honored in the home.

Statuary Standing in Sacred Space

I see a lot of uses for statues in our rituals and our personal magickal devotions. The statue represents something greater than us, and can become a bridging mechanism for communing with the Divine. Statues might be placed at the Four Corners of the sacred space to honor those energies, for example, providing that the Beings represented play nicely together (I typically don't mix pantheons for this reason).

The image of specific beings can also go on your altar when inviting help, giving thanks, or as a simple reminder of your connection to that persona. I often put tokens under or around a statue that represent a specific goal from a spell casting and leave them there until the magick manifests. Sometimes the item remains permanently as an offering (see also Chapter 26.

Making Divine Images

There are so many wonderful suppliers of statuary, including some made by magickal people such as Oberon Zell (*www.mythicimages.com*) that unless you're skilled in some form of carving, you're probably better off shopping for an image that inspires you. If you make that choice, I strongly advocate shopping around in person if possible. As with so many other tools, what something looks like on the Internet and how it feels when you hold it can be very different. Your emotional connection to this tool is very important because of what it represents!

For those who decide to try doing something with clay or wood, take time to meditate on the Divine Being you're representing first. Build a rapport with him or her. While you can get ideas from other artistic renderings, the item you're making is representative of how YOU see this god or goddess. So if you get a completely different idea, trust in your inner vision to guide you.

I would also like to note at this juncture that many images of the Divine have been rough or somewhat indistinct for a reason. In some settings, putting specific attributes on God was considered insulting or limiting (that is, making God in our image). So, even if you're not overly adept with clay, it might be interesting to try your hand at representing the god or goddess of your home in a rough format.

Use clay that won't harden immediately so you can fuss with it a bit. This extra time will give you an opportunity to connect with that being in a different way (tactilely) and think deeply about what that persona means in your home and daily life. Give it a try and afterward place it on your altar, light a candle, and take a moment to be thankful for your blessings.

Post Script

There are certainly many other ways in which we can represent and honor the Divine in our home. Everything from the simple candle and corn dolly to paintings and iconographic symbols is perfectly apt. What's most important here is that each time you see that item it gently reminds you of the Being behind it, and the role that god or goddess has in your magickal life.

Chapter 33

String, Rope, and Yarn

The web of our life is of a mingled yarn, good and ill together.

—William Shakespeare

Some underrated and incredibly useful implements to a Kitchen Witch's tool kit are string, rope, yarn, and thread. These may be used in so many mundane and magickal ways that it is difficult to list them all. In particular, the symbolic value of binding and loosing that such a flexible medium offers has been used by metaphysicians for a very long time. It's this history to which we'll direct our attention.

History Wrapped With a Bow

The making of rope, yarn, and other tying mediums has been lost to prehistory. Nonetheless, we have archaeological evidence of ropes being made in 1700 B.C.E., being braided or twisted. Around 10,000 years ago we find various examples of preserved knots made from plant fibers. This means that materials for tying have been part of human culture basically forever, and along with that long association comes a plethora of magick and superstition.

The first time we find details of various types of knots comes in a medical book of the fourth century. It describes nine different knots for making slings, which of course means that the knowledge for those knots existed long before that tome.

Tip of the Knot

- ٯ According to legend, the Gordian knot was so complicated that no one could untie it. Alexander the Great resolved this problem by slicing the knot with his sword.

- ٯ Square knots are also known as the Knot of Hercules, and it was the most common one used in healing arts for binding sickness, or in tying up wounds so they would heal more quickly.

- ٯ Some sailing ships had special wind knots prepared by sorcerers so that when the winds slowed, magick could whip them up again. This took a traditional form with a rope with four knots (for a light breeze, a steady wind, or a gale). The fourth knot was never to be undone (probably as a symbol of keeping the magick safely within, or a gentle warning against greed).

Across the sea we find both the Incas and Native Americans using knots of a variety of materials for various things. In the case of the former, knots were used to transact business endeavors and as memory aids. For the latter, Native Americans used knots to communicate important dates and as part of story telling traditions. Both of these may have eventually given rise to the idea of a person tying a string around his or her finger so they don't forget!

And what of the infamous Witch's knot? It was a common tool in folk magick that goes back to the middle ages, usually as a charm against Witchcraft! This symbol was etched over doorways to keep negative influences firmly outside. It might also be carried as an amulet.

Making or Buying

Yarn, string, thread, and rope are so inexpensive and abundant that it's not necessary to make your own. I know a few people who spin threads from wool or certain other types of base fibers, and there's certainly symbolic power there (spinning the energy), but these people are few and far between. Personally I'm just as content to pick out a color and texture suited to my goals and get busy.

Applications for Spellcraft and Ritual

For those of you who knit, crochet, tat, or enjoy other related needlecraft, may I recommend a wonderful book by Dorothy Morrison called *Magickal Needlework* (Llewellyn Publications, 2002). It's hard to come by, but is an excellent resource for weaving the magick into your arts in personal and profound ways. It also has a lot more information than I can include in this small space.

For those of you who don't have a talent for such arts, there are still plenty of ways to use these types of tools, including:

- ♋ Binding from harm: A very common old spell but a little on the gray side ethically. Typically accomplished by taking thread or cord (white) and tying it around an image of the person being protected using nine knots.

ᖇ Healing: Take a length of natural fiber yarn or thread and tie it around the part of the body that's affected. Visualize the ailment leaving your body and being bound into the knot. Toss this in running water moving away from you or burn it in a fire-safe area.

ᖇ Healing: For a headache, tie a red piece of string or yarn around your neck very loosely and knot it nine times. Remove it to "remove" the headache.

ᖇ Avert bad dreams: Suspend a knotted string or cord near your bed into which all bad dreams can be gathered before they reach you (this acts akin to a dream catcher, which often has knots in it, made out of sinue).

ᖇ Strengthening a relationship: In Wiccan handfastings, a cord of some type is often placed around a couple's wrists and tied in a lover's knot to symbolize the commitment. Alternatively, you can braid together three pieces of ribbon or cord in colors that symbolize you, your mate, and the relationship. At each area where the three pieces join, tie a knot and/or add an incantation to support the spell. If you can wear this near your heart regularly, all the better.

ᖇ Releasing: When wishing to release someone from a promise, or release yourself from anger, bad habit, etc., you can begin with a piece of yarn or thread in a color that best suits that which you're releasing (a promise might be white, for example). Tie the knot, then ritually loosen it, destroying it afterward.

- ꙩ Safety: Place a knotted cord around the image of an item you wish to protect. White is a good choice. Keep this in a place where it won't be disturbed.

- ꙩ Loosing: Want to release a problem or stress? Concentrate on that while tying knots. Continue until you feel like all the energy of that situation has drained into the cord. Now cut it apart to likewise disperse those energies. Bury the pieces and don't look back.

- ꙩ Wishing: Take three strands of ribbon and braid them into a strand of your hair while thinking of a wish. Wear this until your wish comes true, then untie it with thankfulness.

- ꙩ Divination: An old English custom says that placing a cord with nine knots in it around your bedpost brings prophetic dreams, and of course pendulums function for divination thanks to being suspended by string.

Finally, an idea I got from my children was using a skipping rope and rhymes as a kind of spell. Jump-rope activities date back to the Egyptians. In some areas, doing so was restricted to a male ritual. It's hard to determine exactly why, but we do know even in the 1800s young boys were told about young ladies who burst blood vessels trying to jump rope until exhausted (apparently this was very unlady-like!).

Even so, our notions of such things have changed greatly since then. To me, the energy of the rope moving around you creates a kind of mandala that holds your goal in place until you're ready to liberate the energy you've built up. Think of it as a moving sacred space! Use short rhymes for your incantations all the while you jump, and drop the rope when you release the cone of power!

Off Topic Post Script

The idea of jump roping my way to manifestation also brought up a similar toy to my mind—the hula hoop! Like the jump rope, the hula hoop keeps you in the center of the vortex until your magick is shaped to perfection.

Bibliography

Adler, Margot. *Drawing Down the Moon*. Boston, Mass.: Beacon Press, 1979.

Aldington, Richard, trans. *New Larousse Encyclopedia of Mythology*. Middlesex, England: Hamlyn Publishing, 1973.

Ann, Martha and Dorothy Imel Myers. *Goddesses in World Mythology*. New York, N.Y.: Oxford University Press, 1995.

Arrien, Angeles. Ph.D. *The Four Fold Way*. New York, N.Y.: Harper Collins, 1993.

Bartlett, John. *Familiar Quotations*. Boston, Mass.: Little Brown & Co., 1938.

Black, William George. *Folk Medicine*. New York, N.Y.: Burt Franklin, 1883.

Broth, Patricia and Don Broth. *Food in Antiquity*. New York, N.Y.: Frederick A. Praeger, 1969.

Bruce-Mitford, Miranda. *Illustrated Book of Signs & Symbols*. New York, N.Y.: DK Publishing, 1996.

Budge, E.A. Wallis. *Amulets & Superstitions*. Oxford, England: Oxford University Press, 1930.

Cavendish, Richard. *A History of Magic*. New York, N.Y.: Taplinger Publishing, 1979

Chow, Kit and Ione Kramer. *All the Tea in China*. San Francisco Calif.: China Books and Periodicals, 1990.

Cooper, J.C. *Symbolic & Mythological Animals*. London, England: Aqarian Press, 1992.

Cunningham, Scott. *Crystal, Gem & Metal Magic*. St. Paul, Minn.: Llewellyn Publications, 1995.

———. *Encyclopedia of Magical Herbs*. St. Paul, Minn.: Llewellyn Publications, 1988.

Davison, Michael Worth, ed. *Everyday Life Through the Ages*. Pleasantville, N.Y.: Reader's Digest Association Ltd., 1992.

Decoz, Hans with Tom Monte. *Numerology: Key to your Inner Self*. New York, N.Y., Perigee, 1984.

Delsol, Paula. *Chinese Astrology*. New York, N.Y.: Warner, 1969.

Fox, William, M.D. *Family Botanic Guide*, 18th edition. Sheffield England: William Fox and Sons, 1907.

Gordon, Leslie. *Green Magic*. New York, N.Y.: Viking Press, 1977.

Gordon, Stuart. *Encyclopedia of Myths and Legends*. London, England: Headline Book Publishing, 1993.

Haggard, Howard W. MD. *Mystery, Magic and Medicine*. Garden City, N.Y.: Doubleday & Co., 1933.

Hall, Manly P. *Secret Teachings of All Ages*. Los Angeles, Calif.: Philosophical Reserach Society, 1977.

Hutchinson, Ruth and Ruth Adams. *Every Day's a Holiday.* New York, N.Y.: Harper & Brothers, 1951.

Hutton, Ronald. *Triumph of the Moon.* Oxford, N.Y.: Oxford University Press, 1999.

Jordan, Michael. *Encyclopedia of Gods.* New York, N.Y.: Facts on File, Inc. 1993.

Kieckhefer, Richard. *Magic in the Middle Ages.* Melbourne, Austrailia: Cambridge University Press, 1989.

Kunz, George Frederick. *Curious Lore of Precious Stones.* New York, N.Y.: Dover Publications, 1971

Leach, Maria, ed. *Standard Dictionary of Folklore, Mythology, and Legend.* New York, N.Y.: Harper & Row, 1984.

Leach, Marjorie. *Guide to the Gods.* Santa Barbara, Calif.: ABC-Clio, 1992.

Lurker, Manfred. *Dictionary of Gods & Goddesses, Devils & Demons.* New York, N.Y.: Routledge & Kegan Paul Ltd., 1995.

Magnall, Richma. *Historical and Miscellanious Questions.* London England: Longman, Brown, Green and Longman,1850.

Metzger, Bruce and Michael Coogen, eds.*The Oxford Companion to the Bible.* New York, N.Y.: Oxford University Press, 1995.

Meyer, Marvin & Smith, Richard. *Ancient Christian Magic.* New York, N.Y.: Harper SanFrancisco, 1994.

Murray, Keith; *Ancient Rites & Ceremonies.* Toronto, Canada: Tudor Press, 1980.

Paulsen, Kathryn.*The Complete Book of Magic & WitchCraft.* New York, N.Y.: Signet Books, 1970

Russell, Jeffry R. *A History of Witchcraft.* New York, N.Y.: Thames & Hudson, 1980.

Walker, Barbara. *The Woman's Dictionary of Symbols & Sacred Objects*. San Francico, Calif.: Harper & Row, 1988.

Waring, Philippa. *The Dictionary of Omens & Superstitions*. Secaucus, N.J.: Chartwell Books, 1978.

Wasserman, James. *Art and Symbols of the Occult*. Rochester, Vt.: Destiny Books, 1993.

Websters Universal Unabridged Dictionary. New York, N.Y.: World Syndicate Publishing, 1937.

Index

About the Author

Trish Telesco is the mother of three, wife, chief human to five pets, and a full-time professional author with numerous books on the market. These include the best-selling *Goddess in My Pocket, How to Be a Wicked Witch, Kitchen Witch's Cookbook, Little Book of Love Magic, Your Book of Shadows, Spinning Spells: Weaving Wonders*, and other diverse titles, each of which represents a different area of spiritual interest for her and her readers.

Trish considers herself to be a down-to-earth Kitchen Witch whose love of folklore and world-wide customs flavor every spell and ritual. While her actual Wiccan education was originally self-trained and self-initiated, she later received initiation into the Strega tradition of Italy, which gives form and fullness to the folk magick Trish practices. Her strongest beliefs lie in following personal vision, being tolerant of other traditions, making life an act of worship, and being creative so that magick grows with you.

Trish travels about twice a month to give lectures and workshops around the country. She (and her writing) has appeared on several television segments including *Sightings* on mulicultural divination systems and *National Geographic Today—Solstice Celebrations*. Besides this, Trish maintains a strong, visible presence in metaphysical journals including *Circle Network News*, and on the Internet through popular sites such as *www.witchvox.com* (festival focus), her interactive home page located at *www.loresinger.com*, and Yahoo club *www.groups.yahoo.com/groups/folkmagicwithtrishtelesco*, and various appearances on Internet chats and BBS boards.

Trish has also recently set up a Blog called HOPE (Honoring Other's Positive Efforts) that is "good news, all the time." This is a place to celebrate the acts of kindness, courage, good deeds, and all those shining moments that uplift the human spirit. You can find it at *www.loresinger.com/blog/index.php*

Her hobbies include gardening, herbalism, brewing, singing, hand crafts, antique restoration, and landscaping. Her current project is helping support various Neo-Pagan causes, including land funds for religious retreats.